A Stitch in Time
a true story

Sheila Thomas

AuthorHouse™ UK Ltd.
500 Avebury Boulevard
Central Milton Keynes, MK9 2BE
www.authorhouse.co.uk
Phone: 08001974150

© 2010 Sheila Thomas. All rights reserved.

No part of this book may be reproduced, stored in a retrieval system, or transmitted by any means without the written permission of the author.

First published by AuthorHouse 9/22/2010

ISBN: 978-1-4520-0600-0 (sc)

This book is printed on acid-free paper.

Dedication

For my husband Bob and daughters Julie and Catherine, my son Robert and all my lovely grandchildren.

In memory of my dear son, so sadly missed, Sean Christopher Thomas.

And my father John Christopher Dowling and mother Gladys May Dowling who are forever in my thoughts.

Contents

1.	A Cockney Sparrow	1
2.	Grandmother Charlotte	5
3.	When War Broke Out	12
4.	School Holidays in Ireland	20
5.	My Posh School	23
6.	Will I Meet the Queen at Hartnell's?	28
7.	Nightingales Sing in Berkley Square	32
8.	Rock and Roll	36
9.	I'm Getting Married	41
10.	Goodbye Hartnell's	44
11.	Bob's Birthday Present	48
12.	Twilight Shift	53
13.	The Good Life	57
14.	Now We are Restaurateurs	61
15.	We Lost Rosemary	64
16.	The End of an Era	66
17.	Bob Lost in Arabia	71
18.	Hooray, My Sister is Back	76
19.	My dream Comes True at Last	80
20.	My Worst Fears Become Reality	83
21.	Now - Something to Smile About	88

22. Dawlish Calendar Girls	92
23. My Dream has Ended	97
24. Epilogue	103
25. Acknowledgements	107
About the Author	109

1

A Cockney Sparrow

At last I am writing this book. I've been laid up in bed with a cold virus for several weeks, so have had the opportunity to put pen to paper. Something else has happened to me this year. I've been terminated by a Maltese lady I had been working for for four weeks in the city of Exeter, Devon.

The story begins in 1939 when I was born in London weighing just four pounds. My parents called me Sheila Mary. My daddy was a Southern Irish man, just over from Limerick to make his fortune, when he, Johnny Dowling, met my mum, Gladys May South. Her parents had a little grocery shop in Islington, London. After they married, my Mother and Father took a little flat in Stoke Newington.

1940: Johnny – Sheila - Gladys

It wasn't long before Daddy's sister, my Aunt Mary, came to stay to make her fortune also. She started training to be a nurse, as a lot of Irish girls did in those days. She was only twenty-three, my Mum was twenty and Daddy twenty-six. It was difficult for Irish people to get accommodation in London. Most bed and breakfast houses and flats had notices in their windows stating: *Flat to let. No Irish need apply.*

Dad was working as a Barman in a pub when they started courting. Mum took my lovely Granddad Charlie in to meet him one day and he made the mistake of shaking the wrong Irish Barman's hand! They were both called John and lived over the pub too.

Johnny and Gladys had a short courtship. They got married and decided to apply for their own public house. It wasn't long before Watney's Brewers offered them the George IV in Kentish Town, and so we all moved into the pub.

Then war broke out. My dad was called up to the Army. The Royal Ulster Rifles. He arranged for two young Irish barmaids to come over to England and help Mum run the pub as she was under twenty-one.

My Granddad, Charlie South, a seaman on his last trip before buying a little Inn in Buckinghamshire, was on the London steamer Merel which was struck by one of our own mines on December 8th, 1939 - the beginning of the Second World War. It sank within four minutes and only two of her crew of seventeen were saved. Both were badly injured. A third man was picked up dead.

One of the crew of a motor boat which put out on hearing the explosion stated afterwards that the Merel, which was blown up on the South East coast – in British waters, must have been blown to smithereens. The forepart of the ship had been blown to pieces. No one in that part of the ship could have stood a chance. My Granddad Charlie was at the wheel at the time. My Grandmother and her children, on hearing the news on the radio, were devastated. I was eight months old and cannot remember sitting on my Granddad's knee. My mother told me he was delighted to have a granddaughter.

Granddad Charlie at the wheel of the Merel

2

Grandmother Charlotte

My Nan owned a little terraced house in the village of Tollesbury, Essex, and my two uncles, her two younger boys, worked at a factory, Wilkinsons, in Braintree village. Wilkinsons were famous for making jams and preserves and had a crest on their label. Later in life, when married, I used to look forward to my crate of home made jams from Essex arriving for Christmas and birthdays from Uncle Frank.

My Nan's cottage was small and cosy. The parlour was at the front of the house. We never used that room. The back room was the living room. It was a kitchen and diner, with an old black leather Chesterfield settee and an old coal fire stove and oven. Nan used to sit in front of it summer and winter, making me toast with a long fork against the hot coals. The kettle was always sitting full on the top of the stove. It was war time, and I had bread and milk for breakfast, with Aunt Lil breaking up the pieces of bread, pouring warm milk over the top and sprinkling it with sugar. It was bread and dripping for lunch or sometimes bread and butter sprinkled with sugar. I can also remember being given a spoon full of cod liver oil and malt every day and concentrated orange juice. There were always plenty of tins of condensed milk in the cupboard and dried egg. I liked it.

I was always faking illness to get off school. I liked to lay on the old settee with a blanket over me and staying home with Nan and Lil, and having lots of cuddles. Nan never seemed to go out, always sitting in front of the stove. Lil, on the other hand, did all the house work and shopping. She was a lot younger than Nan. I think Lil must have had a sad romance. I did ask her once and it turned out that the chap was killed in the war and she never married anyone else, living with Nan and Granddad all her life, bringing up all their children. It was she who used to take me out in an old pushchair. We would walk into the village of Tollesbury and shop in the Co-Op. She used to stop and talk to everyone. They all knew Lillian Stevens.

On washing day Lil used to iron the sheets on the big kitchen table. She would put a blanket on the table. The iron would go on the hot plate of the stove, and she had a cover to hold the handle of the iron. She would keep putting the iron back on the range to keep it hot. It took most of the day to iron the sheets, which we would change every week. We had three beds. Denis and Frank slept in the back bedroom and Lil, Nan and I slept in the front bedroom with me being the one to sleep in the middle. There were big knobs on the end of the bed which I often unscrewed and hid things inside!

There was a boiler room outside where the washing was done and a mangle to wring the clothes out. "Could you turn the handle of the mangle while I put the sheets through? But don't put your fingers in," Aunt Lil would say.

All the water would run out of the sheets into a bowl and I would help Aunt Lil hang them on the line. I held the pegs. When we took them off the line I helped fold the sheets. I would hold two corners and walk towards Lil backwards and forwards until the sheets became smaller. I found this a lot of fun.

At the age of three, I used to run down the garden and make Aunt Lil chase me. She would pick me up and put me under her arm. I can remember it hurt my tummy as she ran back to the house with me.

Greeting the milkman when he delivered the milk was a daily occurrence. He used to tease me by pretending to put me in the water butt head first. It was outside the back door and I used to scream and scream. Lil used to say "Milki, put little Sheila down." All I could see were the horrid flies that sat on top of the water. Nan said that rain water was very good for your hair when you wash it. "Oh my gosh," I thought, "I will have flies in my hair!" Every Friday Lil got the tin bath out of the outhouse, put it in front of the fire and filled it with jugs and kettles of hot water for my bath. I used to hope that they were not going to use the 'fly water'.

Everything seems very big when you are so small. We had a greengage tree strong enough for a swing. I was always on it shouting for Uncle Frank or Denis to push it. Denis used to go fishing a lot when he wasn't at school. He must have been on his last year of school when I descended on them. He was tall and lanky. There was a little window at the top of the stairs over the door leading to the kitchen. He used to come downstairs and lift himself up and look through the window at me and pull faces. I used to laugh and laugh. I was only three. After school he worked in the factory with Frank. Then he went into the Army and after the war, back into the factory again. He finally married a local girl and they had three sons. Anyhow, the greengages on that tree were lovely. Frank grew black currants red currants and white currants, raspberries and strawberries.

As I got older Nan let me play with the older children in our road. They would take me for walks in the fields and go bird nesting, and down to Woodrup where the sea was and along an old railway line that was unused. I was only five by then. They used to tease me and run away. We used to play "Germans" in an old Fort by the railway line. In Nan's garden there was an old outside toilet. It was the only one we had. It had to be emptied every so often. I hated it because it was so big and I was so small. I used to worry about falling down into the big hole. We had a commode in the house, I could use that at night because outside was so cold and there were spiders everywhere. Nan used to cut old newspapers into squares and hang them up with string for toilet paper. It was very hard and rough.

My Aunt Lil taught me to knit. I had a little dolly with moveable limbs. She made it a vest. We used to sit and knit most evenings and listen to the wireless. Denis liked to listen to "Dick Barton Special Agent"- it was his special programme. We had a magic lantern with slides. Lil used to set it up at weekends. Lil said it was like going to the pictures. All these treasures were kept under the stairs in a box. I also had a little black dolly and a doll's pram. The lady over the road gave it to Lil for me. It belonged to her daughter, Elizabeth

When my Nan passed away years later, I was married and had four children. I did attend her funeral and I asked what had happened to my dollies, but they were nowhere to be seen. I think someone else in the family took a liking to them. But I would recognise my little baby doll that my aunt made the vest for anywhere. I had so many years of fun with those little toys.

I was sad I couldn't visit my Nan and Lil as often as I liked, but I had four children under the age of six and we lived a long way away. I used to write to Nan and Lil often and make Nan a Bran cake and post it to her. She said it helped her movements down below.

My Nan was one of the old sort who never went out after she was forty. I think the last time she left Tollsbury for an outing was when my Aunt Ivy married. I was four years old. I can remember I wore a little satin dress and a Dutch hat and my mother was a Matron of Honour.

We had lovely woods around Tollsbury and Toleshunt Darcy, and Lil used to take me primrose picking for my birthday. We would fill a basket with these lovely yellow flowers. I was very proud that my birthday fell on 19th April, Primrose Day, but I was glad my parents hadn't called me Primrose. Nan had some little vases. I used to arrange the thin stalks in the water of this little painted green vase which was passed on to me when my Uncle Frank died. It had been passed on to Frank when Lil passed away. I remember it bringing back memories of my childhood in Tollsbury. It's the one thing that reminds me of them and how much I loved them.

On Sundays Frank used to take me to get winkles and shrimps for tea. We used to sit and take the winkles out with a pin and eat them with vinegar and bread and butter. Uncle Frank loved shell fish. We also used to go fruit picking in the season in Toleshunt Darcy, the next village. I'd run around while Lil worked hard strawberry picking. How I loved those summery days. Some years later my Uncle Denis and his wife Barbara moved into a cottage in Toleshunt Darcy. It was owned by my Aunty Lil and was passed down to her from an uncle. The cottage next door was also owned by my Nan and so she and Lil moved into that to be near Denis and family. The other advantage was it had an indoor toilet and bathroom, very modern and very convenient- seeing as my Nan and Aunt Lil were now very elderly.

My Uncle Percy, my Nan's eldest son who was in the Merchant Navy, retired and married an Irish woman and they moved into Nan's old cottage in Tollsbury. They had one son who was born very poorly and never got any better. It was so sad, since my Uncle Percy had always wanted a family. He was very fond of my two little boys. It wasn't long before my Nan's other son, Jack moved to Essex to retire. Now all her sons were around her. All the boys have now passed away. My dear Uncle Frank was the last to go in 2004. He left me a little money,- just enough to build a new kitchen in the house that Bob built. I call it "The Frank kitchen", and I still have the little green vase that sat in my Nan's parlour many years ago. When I look back at those days I have a little smile and I think what a lucky child I was for my first six years as an evacuee.

3

When War Broke Out

My Grandmother moved out of the shop in London and down to Tollesbury, a little town in Essex, with her two younger boys and her sister Lillian. They took me with them. So now I was an evacuee and there I stayed until I was nearly seven. Every so often my Aunt Ivy and her husband Fred would pick me up and take me to stay at the George for the weekend, and that was the time the George always got bombed.

Air Raids were rife when Sheila hit town. I can just remember one Saturday night; I must have been about four years old. The two Irish Barmaids, Winnie and Anne Devany, were behind the bar when the air raid sirens went off. I was grabbed out of my bed and carried down the cellar stairs, along with all the pub's customers, with their glasses still in their hands. One old chap started singing "Roll out the Barrel"! We had a piano down there!

It was a very big cellar. Everyone was snuggled up together. I had a little Mickey Mouse gas mask. That night two houses opposite were bombed to the ground. North London was a target for the Doodle bugs. We had a transport depot opposite the pub and a railway viaduct. There were several factories in our road and one was a plastic factory.

After the all clear, as Winnie carried me up the stairs I could see through the roof. The café on the corner had no windows and the curtains were hanging out. The men came that day and blocked up all the holes in the walls and put wood up where the windows used to be. The poor old George IV looked a sorry sight.

We had a big party at the end of the war. There were trestle tables and benches all down the road. Mum made all the cakes and sandwiches, jelly and things. I had a huge red, white and blue ribbon in my hair. Even the piano was on the pavement. We did the hokey cokey and the conga down to Prince of Wales Road and up again to Homes Road where the Police Station lived. Everyone was so happy.

I started school at the Convent School in Hampstead. I was a bit scared of the Nuns, but Mum used to buy me a big bunch of flowers every Friday to take to school. Patsy Hanes, the Flower Coster, had his stall right next to the bus stop. By the time I was eight he was giving me the flowers for free. I was travelling on my own to school and sometimes the bunch was so big I could hardly hold it. I was still very small for my age. Patsy Hanes and his brother were also very good ballroom dancers and used to give lessons every Friday night. By the time I was thirteen I was quite a good dancer. Mother insisted on my having lessons with the Hanes boys. They looked more like gangsters than dancing teachers, but were typical North London Barrow Boys.

Over the years Mum became a terrific landlady. If some customer was ill she would make sure they had a good dinner and would put it on a tray and deliver it herself to their house. Sometimes at Christmas we never knew half the people around our dinner table. Anyone living on their own was invited to our table.

Lots of Irish relations crossed our door mat over the years; just as well,- they couldn't get accommodation anywhere else. When I finally came home from Essex, Daddy was there and a new baby sister called Maureen.

When I was nine my Uncle Percy bought me a pair of roller skates. I came home from school one day to catch Mum trying them on and skating around the dining club room. My Dad came running up the stairs to see what the noise was about. He said the customers said it sounded like a bus running up and down! He was followed by a Watney's Inspector Man. Luckily he had a good sense of humour.

My Dad's cousin, Donald came to London to make his fortune and stayed at the George all his adult life. Also, Cousin Patrick lived at the George until he married my school friend, Sylvia. Stella came, she was Daddy's niece. She also lived with us from the age of sixteen until she married. I made her wedding and bridesmaids dresses. I had two more sisters: Patricia was born when I was thirteen and Jackie when I was seventeen. My Dad told customers, "Well I'm very partial to girls!" So I had no brothers.

I had to help Mum in our dining room. I had to be waitress on the tables and help wash up. Every Saturday we had a wedding reception. Mum organised it all. She was booked up most Saturdays. I had to help with the wedding breakfast and at the end of the evening I had to help clear up and I always missed the last waltz at the local dance..

In those days the pub closed at 10.30 pm and 10 pm on Sundays, so when I was a teenager I had to be home from a dance by 10.30 pm at the latest to help clean up.

When I was little I used to sit on the stairs and watch the customers in the bar. One Saturday we had a very lively wedding reception, the bride was a Londoner and the Bridegroom Irish. Wow! A big fight broke out between the best man and the groom. Stools were flying and fists. I saw Mum standing on a chair and jumping on a man's back to stop him clocking some chap. I could hear my Dad shout, "Oh Gladys get off his back. Your legs are swinging all over the place and people are bleeding!"

My Dad jumped over the counter. I loved to see him do that he was so good at it! Anyway the Police arrived in no time. Daddy said, "No more Irish weddings. They're trouble."

In the George, my Mum had a cleaner called Lou Bloomfield, who was very partial to a Reid's stout. She said it was good for her health. She was over seventy and was bringing up her grandson Ronnie who was ten years old, and a grand-daughter who was two years old –Doreen. Lou's daughter, called Lois, had been killed during the war in 1942. She worked with her husband Alfred Hughes. He was driving a van pulled by a horse when they were in a collision with a bus and a tram. Poor Louis was killed outright leaving four children motherless. We were told over 500 people attended the funeral with a horse drawn carriage. The horse, called Tom seemed to sense something was wrong and that he would never have Louis to tend to him again. She was most devoted to Tom. Several of her workmates were pole bearers. They were all girls. Louis's four children did not attend the funeral. They were sent off to the country for the day.

Two children were brought up by Lois's parents and two little boys were sent off to Canada to a special school for boys were during the war. Doreen didn't see those brothers again until she was a married woman, and they have since visited England several times over the years. Doreen told me that my mother bought her first school uniform when she joined Junior School. Also when she was eleven my mother told her the facts of life as her Nan never mentioned anything to do with growing up and what to expect. She also said that my mother permed her hair and gave her lots of cuddles when she was sad. She spent a lot of time at the George with us, and most days had dinner or tea with us. I can remember Doreen and me going for a bike ride over White Stone Pond in Hampstead. We had a disagreement and I pushed her and her bike into the pond. She told me years later she got a telling off from her Nan, and I felt really bad.

Doreen was married at the age of eighteen to a lad called David who was in the Royal Navy. We held a reception at the George and my Mum treated her to a two-tier heart-shaped wedding cake and only charged her ten shillings and six pence a head for the reception instead of one guinea. Mum even paid for the band as Doreen and David were paying for everything else themselves. The wedding present from my Mum and Dad was a mangle wringer to go over the sink and Doreen said it came in most handy when she had her first baby just thirteen months later. Doreen and David settled in Portsmouth where David was stationed. They lived in married quarters. A couple of years later, when my husband and I settled in Hampshire, I used to visit Doreen with my babies. We helped them to move when they bought their own house which was only five miles away from us and David joined Bob's wine circle. Old friends are the best and Doreen and David came to my 60th birthday party in Devon. We keep in touch all the time.

When we were about ten years old, my neighbourhood friend Jill and I used to go to Park Road in Camden Town every Saturday to the pet shop. One day we got four white mice. They had lovely pink eyes and white whiskers. I knew Mum didn't like mice, so we had to hide them. We had a spare bedroom at the George. It was Aunty Mary's room. She was a nursing sister on a big ship, the Union Castle Line, and she was in South Africa at the time. She only used the room when she was on leave. So we hid the mice in her wardrobe in a shoe box. Jill and I used to visit the mice every day after school and play with them. One day my Cousin Stella, who lived with us, caught us in the room playing.

"You are not allowed in Aunt Mary's room. What are you doing? I'm telling Aunty Gladys," she shouted. She picked up the box and threw it across the room. The mice went flying, and some landed on the bed. The thing was that Mum just happened to be standing in the doorway!

"What's going on?" she squealed, and jumped on the dressing table. That was the end of that.

The following week we got a lovely white rabbit with pink eyes. Daddy said I could have it in a cage on the roof. It was much nicer to cuddle. The roof was next door to a school where they had evening classes and weight lifting. I was eleven years old and I discovered the glass roof leading from our veranda was the room where the weight lifting took place.

"Don't stand on the glass roof! It's not safe," said Dad, but I wanted to see the boys working out. So I lay down on the glass, spread eagled, watching the boys down below. I was lucky they didn't look up and Daddy didn't catch me!

George IV pub

4

School Holidays in Ireland

My parents were busy people; they used to go to Ireland on holiday every year. I used to have to go and stay there for six weeks on school holidays when I was younger. I loved it- playing in the hay and collecting the eggs and bringing in the cows for milking. You see, we always stayed at Uncle Ned's farm. He was Dad's brother. All Dad's family had farms in Ireland. It was great fun for us kids.

My uncle Ned had ten children. Most Irish families had lots of children, so I had lots and lots of cousins. Mountrath was small town in Southern Ireland fifty miles from Dublin. My Uncle Ned's farmhouse was in a village surrounded by fields called Dysart Beigh. The farm consisted of pigs, cows and chickens. The chickens left their eggs in the hedgerows and all over the place, so we had fun trying to find all them. My uncle Ned and the farm hands used to milk the cows by hand. If I peeped around the door while they were milking, one of them would squirt me in the eye and roar with laughter. I used to love the harvest time, bringing in the hay. We would go with a horse drawn bogie and collect the haycocks one by one. It took hours and then we would make a big haystack. I loved driving the horse myself. The cutting of the corn was a big job. Extra farm hands were taken on and would work all day with a combine harvester, just stopping for lunch, when Auntie Marriead would bring down a basket full of soda bread, ham and cheese and jars of tea. When the day was over everyone would go back to the farmhouse for a big slap-up meal. All the farm hands were invited. Afterwards they would sit around the turf fire playing cards and someone would play a melodeon and sing old Irish songs.

My Aunt Marriead had ten children. She worked very hard. They had a dairy and an old fashioned churn, where she would separate the milk and make cream and butter and also beautiful cheese. I can remember she had no indoor toilet or even a sink. We always used a jug and basin to wash. There was a water pump outside. I cannot imagine how she washed so many nappies and bathed so many children in such dire circumstances. She had no cooker, just a huge turf fire. A big cauldron was placed on a hook over the fire. It was filled with potatoes in their skins. That was the main meal of the day, usually served with gammon.

None of Uncle Ned's children wore shoes during the week, only on Sundays and when they started school. My mother used to send shoes several times a year. Aunt Mary persuaded my mum to send parcels to Ireland, to my Dad's sister. She had a little daughter. They had a pub and a grocery shop in Mountrath. Her husband was a drunkard. I never saw him sober all the time I was on holiday there. Mum used to send my cousin shoes and winter coats, all new. Mary paid for a private school for her sister's child. She helped her sister a great deal.

I also had cousins in Mount Mellick who were publicans. Their business was very big. The pub was at the front, the grocery shop at the back, the slaughter house in the house in the garden, also a brewery. They bottled their own beer. They shot their own bullocks and sold the meat in the shop next door run by my cousin Michael Dowling. They grew their own veg and sold those in the shop. I liked my uncle Mikie and Josie his wife. They had seven children, one was a nun, one a priest and one had a pub. Michael had the butcher's shop while the other girls helped in the business.

One cousin was my age but a real bully. She used to put caterpillars on the range and watch them die. One day she wrapped fly paper around my face. My cousin Attracta told her off. I was very unhappy in that house. She came back to London with me to help my Mum in her pub. She didn't stay long as she missed Ireland. I was pleased to see her leave!

5

My Posh School

My dad was lovely. I used to bring my school pals home from school lunch time for my mum's chips and Dad used to say to them, "Did you know I am a film star?" in that lovely Irish drawl and he used to stand on his head for them. That was his star turn!

My mum was a bit of a social climber. I went from one school to another, the posher the parents the better. I had big birthday parties when all the class was invited, also the parents. We had a big feast and a conjurer and magic man and Punch and Judy. Mum always dolled up. Her dresses almost burst the wardrobe doors open. She had her hair done twice a week, and took me to Selfridges to get my ringlets done. She used to put my hair in grips every night so I had nice ringlets for school. I remember they hurt at night, but I suffered it. I didn't like school dinners. The nuns tried to keep me in the dining room lunch time, but I always escaped. I can remember when I was eight jumping on the bus just as it started up. Sister Mary Agnes was running behind it. She had yanked up her skirt, and I could see her bloomers.

"Sheila Dowling you are a really naughty girl," Sister Mary Agnes shouted.

"Can the driver go faster?" I asked, turning to face the conductor.

Fortunately, I didn't get the cane but she kept me in to do a spelling test. I had to spell *window*, as I was always looking out of it. I didn't pass the Eleven Plus!

When I was twelve, Mum sent me to a convent in Muswell Hill. It was a long bus ride to come home for dinner, so I decided to halve the journey and go to Auntie Ivy's for dinner every school day. She didn't go to work as she had three little children, but she was very fond of me. Anyhow, she cooked the things I liked.

One day I said to her, "Auntie Ivy, everyone at the school speaks French. The teachers are French nuns." She was amazed my Mum would send me to such a school, but the parents were posher than the first school.

One day a relation of Dad's came over from Dublin with his wife and a baby boy called Liam eight months old. They left him at the George and went off to look for work and a flat. I had to look after Liam. He was a nice baby but a bit spotty. Everyone was busy, so I took Liam to school with me. He was a bit large and I wasn't very big for twelve and a half. Anyhow, I sat Liam next to me in class, much to the amusement of the other girls. He was a good baby and slept a lot, so he didn't make much noise. The nun spotted him half way through the lesson and started shouting at me in French, which

I didn't understand and nor did Liam, in fact she woke him up. She pointed to the door, so I guessed she wanted me to leave. Liam was a bit damp anyhow. I was glad to go home. No one asked where I had been and I didn't offer them any information, but I was asked to leave the school. Mum was a bit miffed.

My next school was in Haverstock Hill. Not a convent. Mum was a bit fed up and probably a bit broke by this time. The school was a bit rough. *Secondary Modern* it was called and had boys as well as girls which was a first time for me. One big girl used to trip me up on the concrete stairs. My knees were always bleeding.

"Oh Sheila," my dad would say, "you are always running so fast you trip over your own feet."

"Well, Daddy," I answered, "I think mostly I trip over the Cockney girl's feet."

"Oh Sheila, bring your friend home for lunch," he said, not really listening to me. I thought it might actually be a good idea. "She might like me if she tries my Mum's chips," I thought. So I asked her the next day if she had her dinner money.

"Yes, POSH NOB", was the answer I got.

"Well, why don't you keep it and come home to lunch with me?" I answered. "I live in a big pub and my Mum makes the best chips." And so she did,- every day!

On the way back to school one day she said, "I'm going to my boyfriend's tonight. He's got a TV. We are going to have sex,"

"Oh!" I said, "Not many people in England have TV! He sounds OK, but I don't know about the sex thing. Do you know what to do?"

"Oh yes!" she said. "I've done it lots of times. I might even get engaged!" And she went on to explain the ins and outs of sex.

"Wow!" I said, "I really don't fancy that at all!"

That's how I had my first lesson on it.

We became good mates and then the other girls seemed to like me too. Maybe it had something to do with my dog, Prince. He was a black Labrador and he used to follow me to school every day and wait for me at the school gates until lunch time. Then I'd take him home, along with several other girls, for my Mum's chips and she wondered why I was so popular.

Mum thought I'd better leave that school and go to the North London Polytechnic in Prince of Wales Road, because she knew a girl who had just started there and it would be good for me. I could learn to be a dress designer because I had a good sense of style and tried to make my own clothes.

Sylvia was the girl who showed me around the school. It was very big and very daunting, but I didn't pass the exam, so I had to stay at Haverstack Hill for a bit longer. But Sylvia became my friend, and she used to come home to the George every lunch time for chips. Weekends we used to go up the West End together. She was a year older than me. We used to go to Lyons Corner House, sit upstairs looking out over Piccadilly and order sausages, chips and baked beans, then a Knickerbocker Glory. We did that a lot until Sylvia got interested in my Dad's cousin Patrick who lived with us. She also used to baby sit my baby sister. Anything to see Patrick every day.

6

Will I Meet the Queen at Hartnell's?

It was getting near Easter time and on 19th April, I would be fifteen. What was I going to do with my life? I really fancied going to college to train as a fashion designer. St Martin's was supposed to be the best.

I used to go to Holy Joe's in Highgate to a Youth Club. I liked full skirts, lots of petticoats and little fitted tops. I liked Teddy Boys also. I thought they were smart. My sister Maureen was a Mod by the time she was fifteen and liked Lambretta Scooters and little skirts and jackets.

I loved going to dances as my mother's brother, Jack, was an impresario. He used to run dances at Hammersmith Pally and Hampstead Town Hall. Ted Heath was the Band Leader. We used to dance to big bands. Lita Rosa and Johnny Worth, Dicky Valentine and the likes were singers, but I always missed the last dance as I had to be home for 10.30 pm to help clean up the Reception room of the Saturday Wedding.

One Saturday before Easter there was a very big wedding at the George. The Bride looked stunning! I had never seen such a lovely dress. As Mum and I were listening to the speeches, the groom said he was very impressed with the lovely reception Mum had put on and they clapped us as we were looking through the serving hatch of the kitchen.

"Wow! What a dream dress!" I said to Mum. "I wonder where she got it from? I'd love to be able to make something as good as that!"

At the end of the night Mum spoke with the bride. "My little Sheila loves your dress. Where on earth did you get it? We have seen hundreds of weddings over the years and have never seen anything so lovely."

"Well," she said, "I work for Norman Hartnell in Bond Street. He trained me and now I am one of his top couturiers. The House of Hartnell made all the gowns for the Queen and Royal Family for the Coronation, including the Queen's wedding gown. We are the top designers and makers in England. Norman Hartnell was here at the reception and was very impressed with the service you gave. When does Sheila leave school? Would she like an interview at Hartnell's?"

And so my dream came true. I got the job! I didn't even have to do an exam, just take a bit of my own dressmaking to show I was capable. I lay in bed before my first day at work and dreamt I would be answering the phone to the Queen. I would say, "Yes, Mam. Of course I can make an appointment for you!" But my apprenticeship didn't include answering any phones.

I was nearly fifteen and my wages were thirty-nine shillings or about four pounds per week, which didn't leave much over for dancing. There were about thirty people in our workroom; eight of them were apprentices and assistants, three to a table, the older girl about twenty-one, her assistant about eighteen and the apprentice fifteen – sixteen. I was the youngest there.

I soon made friends with Beryl. She was sixteen and had just started the same day as me. We used to go to the coffee bars after work to Wardle Street to the *2 Eyes* where Tommy Steele played his guitar and sang. We used to jive together in the basement. I would clip clop down the cobbled mews of Bruton Street off Bond Street in my little stiletto shoes, my big full skirt and little top. One day the elastic went on my petticoat and the lot fell down around my ankles.

My friend Maureen, who was a neighbour and used to travel to work with me on the tube, just fell about laughing. She was a milliner and worked for the Queen also. We were both fifteen and thought we were both so grown up. "That petticoat has too many frills on it. It must weigh a ton," she said as I picked it up and flung it over my arm.

When I looked up I could see a lady with big pink hair standing outside the back entrance of Hartnell's talking to a rather stern woman of around thirty to forty. It was Barbara Cartland talking to her daughter Raine. I could never understand why they always came in the back door. Maureen and I both burst into giggles of hysteria.

If I was an important person I would have used the front entrance of Hartnell's. It was so impressive with its big pillars and lovely windows. It fronted on to Berkely Square where the nightingales sing.

Norman Hartnell and girls in the workroom

7
Nightingales Sing in Berkley Square

One day Maureen and I took our lunch and sat in Berkley Square in the gardens. As we sat on the bench Maureen said to me, "Look over there! That's Bing Crosby! He's famous!"

We saw lots of famous people where we worked. Laurence Harvey had a Mew's house right opposite the back entrance of Hartnell's. He used to lean out his window in the mornings as we were coming to work, and whistle at Avril, the girl who was training me. She was very pretty and very tall. She was twenty-one and I looked up to her. She was one of Hartnell's best dressmakers.

The Head of our workroom was Miss Alice, who I suppose was about fifty, - I think, when you are fifteen everyone over twenty-two is old!

Each season Mr Hartnell and Captain Mitchison used to design the collection for the three workrooms for five models. He would bring the designs into the workroom and talk the collection through with Miss Alice. She would make the pattern on a dummy and then the head dressmaker would help cut it out. There were about ten hands (couturiers) as Hartnell liked them called. Her assistant would help tack it up for the first fitting and then her apprentice would take it down to the fitting room for a fit on the chosen model (all the models at Hartnell's were over six foot tall and a size ten). Norman Hartnell would have to see it and approve of it and make any changes he wanted while it was unfinished. There were between fifty and a hundred gowns each season.

Our workroom was at the top of the building with bare floorboards and one toilet between thirty people. We had one ironing board and one table to iron on. There was only one electric iron; all the others were flat irons. We had to put them on a gas ring to heat and then duck them in a bucket of water before using. All the sewing machines, all three of them between thirty Couturiers, were treadle or wind up, no electric machines like nowadays. Remember this was 1955. I was told by my betters in the workroom, "Sheila, don't complain about the machines. All the Coronation gowns were made on them and you can't get better than that."

A lot of work was done by hand, only the seams were machined. They were all hand over-sewn. There were no over lockers at all. All the hems were done by hand. That's why we were called Couturíers. As an apprentice I had to watch and learn. I had to pick up any pins dropped on the floor, make shoulder pads and padded hangers to match the gowns and do shoulder clips for most gowns. I could work on the linings and do my neatest button holes all by hand – gosh, I had to run about.!

When the gowns were all made for the fashion show, Mr Hartnell saw the rehearsal and approved or disapproved. Then the Queen attended on her own with one lady in waiting and Mr Hartnell. The Queen would choose which gowns she wanted for the season or for a tour she had to go on. Those gowns were then taken out of the Collection since no one else ever had a copy of the Queen's gowns. Mr Hartnell would have to put more gowns into the Collection to replace the lost gowns, and then we were ready for the big Fashion Show.

The Show Room was beautiful, with thick carpets, mirrored walls and lots of marble and velvet chairs. All the apprentices from the three workrooms would bring down all the gowns on the morning of the Fashion Show. The other two workrooms were headed by French ladies and the sales ladies were called vendeose. Their assistants were all debutantes, daughters of Lords and Ladies, with no commoners like us little girls upstairs. The debutantes had all been presented to the Queen. The girls I worked with told me that every Christmas the Queen used to put on a big party for the Hartnell workers in Buckingham Palace. But just after the Coronation that all changed, and so there were to be no more parties for the Hartnell girls. So Sheila missed out, "Boo hoo!" The year I started at Hartnell's the party was cancelled!

We started work on the Queen's gowns for her Australian tour. Most of her fittings were done at the Palace, and Miss Alice had to attend with Mr Hartnell. The big Fashion Show was fun for us apprentices. Elizabeth Taylor, Barbara Hutton, members of the Guinness family and other big names were in our Show room. When it was all over, and the models went home, we collected up all the gowns and put them away, but only after we had marched up and down the catwalk pretending we were models! We pretended to chat to the film stars and the like as we tripped over long long gowns and fell out of size seven shoes!

In the evening Beryl and I went for a coffee at the *Le Macarbe*, the *Heaven and Hell*. We used to buy our underwear at Williz on Shaftesbury Avenue. That's where all the showgirls got their frillies! One month I saved up and bought a red silk pantie suspender belt and bra. Friends were round the George one night and pinched my knickers - which were on the clothes horse in front of the fire.

I didn't notice until I was crossing the road the next morning to get the tube because at Kentish Town, one of the boys threw my knickers at me in the middle of the road on the zebra crossing. I went as red as my knickers!

One morning on my way to work, with my little friend Maureen, we turned off Bond Street into the cobbled mews. My little white stilettos, click clicked on the cobbles. Oh dear, I caught my heel in a little gas manhole cover. I couldn't move. I tried to lift my foot and the manhole cover moved along with me. The gentleman behind us in his bowler hat and his long umbrella tut tutted as Maureen and I imagined him falling down the hole. We giggled so much! Workmen on the side of the road had to release my shoe so we could continue on to work. Maureen often reminds me of that day and we giggle about it even now.

8
Rock and Roll

On Thursday nights they had rock & roll at the Lyceum in the Strand. Bill Hayley was the band and so Beryl and I put on our glad rags and were looking forward to a great night out. I was eighteen, Beryl nineteen. We got a drink and sat up in the balcony watching the boys below. Two young men were hunched up at the bar looking all around. One was very dark with curly hair, in a black suit; the other was fair and much taller.

"Oh, they look alright! Beryl said. The dark one will be too short for me, but I think he's giving me the eye!"

Anyhow they saw us and we had a good giggle about it. "Will they, won't they come up here?" we debated.

Oh yes! They did! The dark one was Bobby and he bought me a drink; the blonde one was for Beryl. They seemed to be very nice and had lots of money. Bobby was very brown because they were both in the Merchant Navy and were on leave. I spent the whole of Bobby's leave with him in the evenings. I introduced him to Mum and Dad and they even let him take me to an all-night party. They seemed to trust him, although my Dad was a bit worried because Bob was so dark.

"Have you seen his legs? he said to my mum. "They are like a darkies!"

"Yes, but his parents are Scottish and come from Glasgow, although now they live in Brighton!" my Mum replied.

My Dad liked Bob because he was good behind the bar. He worked for the New Zealand Shipping Company and travelled to New Zealand and back. He had been in the Merchant Navy since he was sixteen and had worked his way up to barman. He had been all around the world twice by the time he was twenty. He was away for four months and four weeks at home. We carried on seeing each other for eighteen months. Beryl's chap disappeared. Bobby said he jumped ship in New Zealand. Beryl started going out with the boy who lived next door called Ron.

We were busy at Hartnell's, and I was learning a lot. Princess Margaret used to come in for her fittings for the gowns she chose from the fashion show. She had just split up with Peter Townsend, who we all know she was in love with, but the Queen did not approve because he was a divorced man. I was now an assistant to Avril and we had an apprentice called Shirley. I was upset to see the Princess so sad. Sometimes she came into the fitting room quite drunk and I was so happy with my Bobby. I felt sorry for her.

Norman Hartnell started to go into cosmetics, selling soaps and the like. The soaps were pink and in the shape of hearts. I used to buy them as presents for members of my family. On my mum's birthday, May 2nd, I treated her to a very large box of heart soaps.

"You can get them from Mr Hartnell's apartments," Miss Alice told me. "Just knock on his door. His secretary will give you a box."

Mr Hartnell had a lovely apartment down a flight of stairs near our workroom, overlooking Berkley Square. So I put on some fresh lippy and tapped on his door and who do you think opened it? Norman Hartnell himself! He looked down at me and smiled.

"What's your name?" he asked. "I think I know you, little girl."

"I'm Sheila Dowling," I answered. "You came to a wedding reception at my parents' pub over three years ago and now I work for you. I'm an assistant now."

"Well Sheila Darling, what would you like?"

"Three in love soaps," I heard myself say. And that's how I got introduced to the man himself, as my Daddy would say!

One day the Queen surprised us all by visiting the showroom for a viewing of some suitable gowns because she was pregnant with Prince Andrew. I had to take several gowns to the fitting rooms for her to see. She was wearing a lovely green velvet coat and had Princess Ann and Prince Charles with her. They were very rude and were fighting on the floor. Mr Hartnell nearly fell over them.

"Get off me you bitch," I could hear Ann say to Charles.

I told the other girls in the workroom I thought it was a stupid thing to say, but she was only a kiddie and so ill behaved. The Queen told them both off.

Over the next few years four girls in our workroom got engaged. Beryl was one, I was one and Avril and Peggy. Princess Margaret got engaged to Anthony Armstrong Jones and Norman Hartnell was commissioned to design the gown. We all wondered who would make it. I was quite ill for a while. I went to Ireland on holiday and when I came back I was in so much pain in my legs I couldn't walk. I had rheumatic fever and ended up in Hampstead General Hospital for some time. When Bobby came home on leave, I had just got out of a convalescent home. Bobby asked my dad's permission to marry me and he took me to Brighton to meet his little Mum, Agnes, and his big Dad, Bob. Being Scottish, they celebrated New Year's Eve and we had a great time. We planned to marry in August.

Peggy was working on Princess Margaret's wedding gown. We all got a chance to a bit of work on it. I cut off a bit of my hair and sewed it into the hem. At least my hair would be walking down Westminster Abbey, even if I wasn't! Princess Margaret told Mr Hartnell she wanted her bridesmaid's dresses to be a copy of a little dress her Father loved her in. It was pale blue organza and had tucks in the skirt and bodice. I was chosen to make one of the eight dresses. What an honour! She married at Easter time. Mr Hartnell arranged for a television to be installed in our workroom so we could watch the wedding live and see all our hard work displayed to the world.

The wedding of Princess Margaret and Anthony Armstrong Jones was so wonderful! The bride had eight brides-maids. Her dress was quite stunning. It was as if she moved in a soft white cloud. The thirty yards of fabric was of fine diaphanous silk with a fitted bodice and a "V" neckline. The skirt was of twelve panels, a deep inverted pleat let into the centre back at the waist line allowed the dress to be folded when the bride sat down, and then fall back into place when she stood up, so no unsightly creases would show. Princess Ann was her Chief Bridesmaid and her gown was a copy of a dress worn by Margaret at her first ball aged seventeen and it was her father's favourite. She arrived at the ceremony in a glass coach, escorted by the Household Cavalry. The Duke of Edinburgh gave her away. She must have been so sad not to have her father by her side, because she obviously loved him very much.

Royal Wedding

9

I'm Getting Married

I was now twenty-one. Bobby left the Merchant Navy because he said he needed to train for a trade, seeing as we were to be married. He did not discuss it with me, but he joined the Army, the R.E.M.E. He said they would train him to be an electronic engineer and it was a good trade and well paid. I wasn't very keen on being a soldier's wife, but I went along with it.

Beryl married in July and I was a bridesmaid. Avril also married in July. They were lovely weddings. I was told it was unlucky to make your own wedding gown, your trainer makes it for you, but you can make your own bridesmaids dresses. My three sisters were to be maids and my friend Jill, Maid of Honour, as Maureen the milliner was already married and pregnant. Sylvia married Patrick, and cousin Stella, who also lived at the George, got married in 1959. It was a lovely year and I made most of the dresses.

The Banns were called at St Dominic's Priory in Hampstead for August 6th 1960 Sheila Mary Dowling was to wed Robert Beith Thomas.

My dress was wonderful. I had to ask Norman Hartnell if I could use one of his designs I had fallen in love with. The gown was one he had designed for Princess Margaret for her engagement to Anthony Armstrong Jones. It was a pale pink ball gown, but I wanted to make it into a Bridal Gown in white. I knocked on Mr Hartnell's apartment door, tap, tap, and he answered it himself.

"Well, well! Sheila Darling," he exclaimed, "is it love soaps again for your Mother?"

"Oh no, Sir," I said. "I want to discuss my wedding gown with you."

I must say in all the times I have spoken to him I have never corrected him when he called me Sheila Darling instead of Sheila Dowling. I rather liked it.

Mr Hartnell picked up a pencil and pad and started to draw. "What would you like my dear?"

"I know just what I want," I told him and I described the gown.

"But it's pink," he said

"Yes Sir. Can we change it to white?"

"Yes of course, but it is a strapless boned rouched bodice. Can't show your shoulders off on your wedding day, Miss Darling," he said. "We will have to have a lovely lace overlay bodice with fitted sleeves. Wouldn't that be lovely?"

And so, even after forty-seven years, people are still talking about that wonderful gown.

Beryl couldn't come to the wedding because she was still on honeymoon. I made a good job of the four Bridesmaids dresses, all in sky blue with puff ball skirts. Patsy Haynes did me some lovely bouquets, Princess Elizabeth roses and Lily of the Valley.

When I left the pub for the church, the whole pavement was lined with the George IV customers I'd known since I was a baby, - even the coal man and lorry drivers. My Dad was so proud. He was so nervous he nearly ran me up the aisle! My baby sister Jackie was only four years old and looked really cute. Mother looked grand in a lovely cream lace dress made by Peggy at Hartnell's.

Sheila in bridal gown

10

Goodbye Hartnell's

We went to Jersey for our Honeymoon. I had to leave Hartnell's because Bobby had been transferred to Gloucester. We were in the Army now. I didn't like Army life. I was so home sick. We were not in Army accommodation as we had a little private flat just outside the town.

Mum sent my little sister, Jackie, to stay with us since she had started school and was on summer holiday. Anyhow, I was pregnant and my baby was due in August.

When our baby boy arrived my Daddy was over the moon. The first boy in our family. He was so special. We called him Robert. But I couldn't wait to leave Gloucester. Two years later I was pregnant again and the baby was due in November. Bobby was being posted to Aden as there was a war going on there. He was due to leave in December, so we moved to London and stayed at the George so I could have the baby there and Mum and the family would look after me while Bob was in Aden. Robbie was only two years old. He was not very well behaved a lot of the time. I was always running after him. One day he tipped six bottles of milk into the fridge to make a pond and floated bits of cheese and sausages in it. He piled up all the saucepans along the hall and made balls out of the toilet paper, which he soaked in the toilet first and then aimed down the stairs, just missing customers' drinks.

My confinement was arranged with a midwife from Holloway, the same Polish lady who delivered my baby sister Jackie.

On November 27th Mum and Dad were preparing for an Express Dairy function in the Club room. In the morning I was helping Daddy make sausage rolls and sandwich fillings for the evening, Robbie was having a little nap after lunch. The two and a half year old had worn himself out since he got up.

"Time out," I said to Daddy. "I will make you a cup of tea."

I put my hand in the kitchen unit for a bag of sugar and low and behold a pair of eyes was looking out at me. It was a mouse. The George had lots of mice. They came up through the skirting boards. I hated them. You have never seen me move so fast. I jumped up on to the draining board and put my feet in the sink. Daddy was quite alarmed. After all, my baby was due on 28 November and this was the 27th.!

"Oh Sheila you shouldn't be doing that and you being pregnant, so you are!"

I was laughing and crying at the same time. Bobby was on duty at Gloucester Camp before his move to

Aden. I was looking forward to him coming home that weekend. I had a bit of a rest in the afternoon while my Sister Maureen looked after Robbie.

I walked into the kitchen as she was chatting to Robbie. "What does he want, Sheila?" she asked. "He's tapping the top of his head and saying "top of my ted, top of my ted?"

"Oh sweetie, he wants a drink full up to the top, not a little one," I told her.

The Express Dairy do was in full swing. My Mum was very busy and Dad was in the bar. Our milk man Joe was in there with his wife Hilda, and then I went into labour! I found Mum and told her the pains had started and asked her to call the midwife. But, no way! She was too busy!

Then my waters broke! Oh dear, someone was in a hurry, so I found my milkman's wife and asked her to call the midwife, and then it started to snow.

The midwife arrived on her bike in the snow shouting her orders. Mum and Dad were getting rid of the rest of the Party. It was midnight. I was grateful that Robbie slept so well. Mum wanted to be with me when baby arrived, but she squeezed my hand so hard my rings were cutting into my fingers and I screamed, so the midwife sacked her.

My darling little boy was born, he was only four pounds. Mum wrapped him in a towel and showed him to Daddy and the barmen and the barmaids and then I went to sleep.

I phoned Bobby in the morning and gave him the news. Robbie had a brother. Seań Christopher was here.

Now I had two little boys to look after. Robbie was a little pickle, but Seań was a good baby. We had a good christening in London and then Bob was off to Aden with the Army. At the end of his tour Bob was demobbed. Soon he was offered a job in Hampshire with *Plessy*, as an Electronic Engineer. He still had to go to college, but Plessy would give him a day release to college to get his HNC qualifications.

We put a deposit on a lovely little house in Lovedean village in Lovedean Lane, in Hampshire, not far from Portsmouth. When Seań was 12 months old I was pregnant again.

Bob enjoyed working for Plessy. I made a lot of friends in the village and joined a keep-fit club. The baby was due on Bob's birthday, 7th November. We always visited Bob's parents in Brighton on his birthday and this year was no different.

11

Bob's Birthday Present

His Mum was concerned because the baby was due soon, so we didn't stay the night and made tracks for home. I put the boys in their pyjamas in the car. On the way home my waters broke, "Are we nearly there?" I was tempted to say.

Well, thank God, we were almost there! Bob picked up Robbie and tucked him into bed and then came back for Seań and tucked him into bed. I made my way upstairs to prepare for the midwife to arrive. But the baby was in a hurry and started to come before the midwife, so Bob had to help do the delivery! It's the first baby Bob had been in time to see delivered. He was so excited as her head popped out just as the Midwife arrived.

"It must be a girl," said Bob, "she has her eyes wide open and she's not out yet."

From that day on she was very special to Bob.

In the morning he brought our two little boys in to see their sister. I made a fuss of Seań as he was so young and I didn't want him to be jealous as he wasn't the baby any more.

"She is your baby, just as you were Robbie's baby," I told him. "What would you like to call her?"

"She will be Twinkle" he said, and she *was* - for at least 6 weeks!

We now had a TV in our house. Bob didn't really approve, but I loved it. We always had a TV at the George, so I rented one and did dressmaking at home to pay for it. The boys loved the children's programmes and Seań loved music. His favourite singer was a little blonde girl called "Twinkle" – surprise, surprise!

We decided to call the new baby Julie Ann as it was the same as my midwife and we couldn't agree on any other name. It suited her, anyhow. She looked like Bob's side of the family with dark eyes and dark hair. The boys were blonde, with blue eyes like my family, in fact Robbie was strawberry blonde, Seań was darker.

Bob joined a wine circle and used to make his own wine. He'd pick the fruit and sometimes we would all help by strawberry picking if the boys didn't eat them all first. He even made his own beer. We had a big black bin under the units and loads of Demi Johns. We used to have a lot of parties as the footballers of Portsmouth were neighbours of ours. I used to give dress parties for the wives. It was great fun.

One Sunday we were getting ready for church and Seań was being difficult. Every time I put his shirt on, he would take it off. We finally got the three of them in the car and into church. Seań was very lively. We all noticed that the Priest had had his hair cut. The week before it had been very long.

Seań whispered in my ear, "Mummy, Jesus has had a haircut" and he giggled. I looked at Bob. Oh my, Seań's breath stank of beer! We couldn't understand where he got it from. He kept saying it was Daddy's big mug to blame. We put him to bed early and he was quite alright the next day.

We couldn't find Bob's big mug anywhere – not that is, until two weeks later when Bob was siphoning his beer back from the bin to the bottles and we found the big mug at the bottom of the bin. Little Seań must have been sweeping the froth off the top of the bin with the mug and drinking it when he dropped it. What a good job he didn't fall in himself, but he never touched the beer again. He said it gave him belly ache!

When Julie was eighteen months, I was pregnant again and Catherine Jane from Lovedean Lane was born on August 26th and that was the last little Thomas. I had a little operation as we now had a big enough family.

I had four children under six years, a lot of work, and then had rheumatic fever again. I worried about the kiddies if I was in hospital for a long while, but all my friends rallied around and took it in turns to look after my brood. They did the washing, ironing, child minding, and Gloria, my hairdresser friend, even did the girls' hair as it was very long. We all pulled together and I made a full recovery.

My husband enjoyed his meetings at the wine circle and enrolled two friends, who also got the bug for making wine. The meetings were held in old tea rooms which were owned by friends who ran the circle. Sometimes wives were invited to a social evening tasting each other's wines. One evening we had a Murder in the Dark party. It was so funny wandering around in the dark in this old café. We also had competitions for the best wine.

One evening a month Bob would invite all the chaps around to our house for wine tasting and it also progressed into beer making and tasting.

I got home from a dress party to find all these men passing the baby around the room. Julie was only five months old and seemed to enjoy it very well. I only hoped she wasn't breathing all their alcoholic fumes.

Bob was very friendly with the Portsmouth Footballers. They lived in our village. We used to give parties for them on a regular basis. Their wives belonged to my Keep-Fit Club. Pat Hand, one of the wives, used to come with me to London once a month to buy party dresses to sell on a stall in the Football Club grounds on a Sunday. All the wags (footballers wives), would buy the gowns to wear at the Jokers Club and the Playboy Clubs on our various nights out.

On one trip to London we were going down the King's Road in Chelsea and Pat spotted George Best and Pat Jennings. They were friends of her husband Oien. We were invited back to George's house in Chelsea for coffee. I didn't realise he was famous then.

At home we had four space hoppers for the children and the footballers used to love racing each other down our garden on them. I had to invite our neighbours in case we made too much noise and they were very impressed with our guests. They were the best parties!

12

Twilight Shift

The girls loved singing and dancing and I enrolled them in a drama group. The boys belonged to the Nautical Training Core, which Bob helped to run, as the children were now at school. I started an evening job with Estee Lauder. They did a twilight shift at a factory in Petersfield. A coach was put on to pick people up from surrounding villages and towns. It was so convenient and I really enjoyed it. Working in a factory was a new experience for me as I had only worked for Norman Hartnell. The girls there were very feisty and loud. We used to fill the pots with face cream on a conveyor belt that moved quite fast and if you didn't keep up you could get covered in cream. At the end of the evening the girls used to take it in turns to sit on the end of the conveyor belt, they said the vibration gave them a nice feeling in the nether region. What naughty girls! I loved all the products and had a go at making lipsticks, powders and even bottling perfumes. I was promoted to a Quality Control Inspector and I was very proud of myself.

Bob was doing very well at *Plessy* and was promoted to Chief Engineer. We were in a position to make an extension on our house as the boys were getting bigger. We needed an extra bedroom, so we built a double garage with 2 bedrooms over and another bathroom. The house next door was owned by Gary Glitter's cousin. We were invited to a party there one evening. We put the kiddies to bed and a baby sitter was installed. The boys' bedroom overlooked the garden next door, and Seán said he could see all the pretty coloured lights in their garden. So we were having a garden party, were we? It all went swimmingly well, nice music and plenty of food. We didn't really know anyone there. We seemed to be the only ones in Lovedean Lane invited. Bob and I were amused to see people climbing the trees and swinging from the branches, but when they started taking their clothes off, we made a run for it over the hedge.

Next day Seán said, "Mummy that was a funny party you went to, they had monkeys in their trees!"

My parents wanted to go to Ireland on holiday for two weeks, so Bob and I said as it was the school holidays; we would run the pub for them if they took Robbie and Seán with them. It seemed a good deal and I thought the boys would love that. The night before the trip to Ireland Daddy was so excited. He loved the idea of taking his two grandsons to meet all the relations. When the pub was closed Mum ran the bath for Daddy. We could hear them in the bathroom splashing about.

"It sounds as if they are in the bath together!" I said to Bob. We were quite shocked, but after all my parents were still young.

I remembered just after we had Robbie, it was my parents 25th Wedding Anniversary. My little sister Jackie was only five and Patricia was ten. Maureen was married and pregnant. We all went to the Talk of the Town in the West End to see Shirley Bassey. It was a lovely evening for the family.

Bob enjoyed running the pub and I made snacks for the bar in the lunch time. The pub closed for a short break between three and five in those days. Bob was clearing up and Julie Ann was running about singing through the microphone and dancing when all of a sudden she fell off the stage.

Bob screamed up the stairs to me, "Help, help! I think she has electrocuted herself."

Her lips were blue and she was unconscious. I called an ambulance. The words hardly came out, but it wasn't long before the ambulance came. I picked up Cathy Jane and I was so shocked because I thought we had lost Julie, but she came too and she was sick. "Oh thank God." She spent a few days in hospital. It seems she had had a convulsion because she was so hot. I had previously taken them in the pram to Camden Lock. It had been a hot day and she had got over heated. I had learnt a lesson I would always remember.

I was pleased when Mum and Dad returned from Ireland and we could go home again. I missed my boys so much. Seán told me he had to share a bed with five other cousins at Uncle Ned's.

"I had to share a bed with a lot of cousins when I was little," I said.

"Yes," he answered, "but I bet you didn't wet the bed!"

The next holiday we had was to Spain. Bob's Mum and Dad had moved there and we liked it so much that every school holiday we put the children in the car and set off for the ferry. We would drive all the way over the mountains to Benicia in Spain. The children loved it! They were all like little water babies! Bob's Mum and Dad, Agnes and Bob, liked the life in Spain and lived there for about ten years.

Robbie and I appeared in the film *Tommy*, directed by Ken Russell. The Who and Roger Daltry were the stars. Keith Moon was a riot! He broke guitars and threw drums all over the place. We rubbed shoulders with Elton John and Oliver Reed, who was also very interesting. Robbie and I were only extras, but we enjoyed it very much.

13

The Good Life

When Cathy, our youngest, was about nine and a half we decided to move to Devon. Bob wanted to live the good life. He had this dream of growing his own vegetables and fruit and opening a green grocers shop. Needless to say, I wanted a dress shop, but Bob won and off we went. Robbie didn't want to come. He went to London to stay at the George with Mum and Dad and started a little job with Kodak as he was interested in photography. I was upset. I wanted to keep my family together.

We put a deposit on a Small Holding in Holcombe, between Dawlish and Teignmouth in South Devon. It had seven bedrooms and three quarters of an acre of land with thirty fruit trees. We also rented a new green grocers in Teignmouth. We had a lease for several years.

The children settled into the schools. Julie and Seán were in Torquay and Cathy in Teignmouth. Julie and Seán didn't like the school very much and told the Headmaster what they thought of it. Julie looked over the Secondary School in Teignmouth and they both enrolled themselves there and were very happy.

It was soon my sister, Jackie's 21st birthday and I went to London on my own for her party. I talked Robbie into coming to Devon. I missed him so much. He quite enjoyed his life in Devon. He got a motor bike and so life was better for him. But it wasn't long before he joined the Army. The green grocers wasn't doing very well. There were several other greengrocers in Teignmouth. Bob said we could be different by growing most things ourselves and then buying from the market instead of having stuff delivered from distributors, and the market would be cheaper anyhow. We had a very old van, in fact it had no floor in the back, so all the crates had to go on the roof rack. An old man used to help Bob and go to market with him; they also liked to go fishing together.

At home we had no washing machine, no cooker, no fridge, only an old Rayburn which also heated the water. There was no central heating and the chimney of the Rayburn was disintegrating with the heat and it was rusty!

How I wished I had the mod cons I had had back in Lovedean, but the kids didn't seem to mind. They just put another jumper on in the winter. Cathy loved animals and made friends with Rosanna, a neighbour, who lived in a big house with horses and wallabies and all sorts of animals like chipmunks and silkies. We had a cat and four kittens and a dog called Bella which Seań brought home one day, but he never seemed to take her out for walks. I had to. In fact she used to take me down to the beach at the end of our road. She was a Collie cross- breed and was very beautiful. One day I discovered eight kittens. Cathy had acquired four more from the house up the road as the man was about to drown them.

Julie had a little evening job in a hotel. Bob got her a scooter to travel to work. But she kept falling off it. So Cathy used to follow her to work to make sure she was okay. Cathy had a motor bike. She was a tomboy!

Things were not going very well at the greengrocers. We didn't make enough money to keep three teenagers. They were all still at school, but their pocket money came from the little jobs they had. Seań and his pal, John Dumper, used to sell fish to the pubs. I don't know where they got them from. John used to have Seań push the cart around town and John would do the talking and selling. Both boys were into music and dressed like Rockabillys. Seań and John Dumper were photographed for a magazine. They were in the Purple Penny amusement arcade playing the machines when the photographer photographed them as two typical teenagers of Devon Rockabillys. The photo was ace and published in a top magazine. The boys called themselves the Duke and the Earl. They were not into drugs or drink - just music.

Bob and I used to help run a disco for them on Saturday nights in the local theatre. Julie had a boyfriend called Chris and Cathy had Kevin Robbins chasing her around. The girls were only thirteen and fifteen.

Then Bob found a job in Arabia. It was good money but I had to run the greengrocers on my own. I had the old man to drive the van to the market once a week but I had to get on the roof and load the crates up there. The market traders must have wondered why we didn't put it in the back of the van, but if we did it probably would have fallen through the floor.

I kept the greengrocers stocked with fresh vegetables and fruit every day and at last I sold the lease of the shop. I paid off what we owed and bought a gas cooker and fridge and also an old car, so that when Bob got home he could have wheels to look for a job.

When Bob finally came home he was not pleased I had spent the money from the sale of the shop, but I thought it was better than having the shop empty, and walking away from it all - although I often felt like it.

14

Now We are Restaurateurs

We took on a short lease on a restaurant in Teignmouth. I really loved the building. It was on the Point. We had the river to the back of the building and the sea to the front. It was called "Riverside." It had a little kiosk on the front which Bob put Seań in charge of. He had to sell fish and chips and burgers and all that sort of fast food, also ice cream. He told everyone he was the Manager. I remember the first piece of fish he fried. The oil must have been too hot, because the fish shrunk inside the batter and the irate customer brought it back. Poor Seań was so embarrassed.

We opened at six in the morning at the café because Bob discovered that the ships docked behind Riverside and the sailors were wandering around town looking for breakfast.

If we sat up in bed we could see the ship docking, so out he jumped and put the cooker on and expected me to follow him. Bella, our dog, was now even nearer the beach since the beach was on our door step. Bella used to jump out of the window and one day slid down the slope behind on to the beach, followed by all the other dogs in Teignmouth seeing as she was on heat.

One day Bob took Bella for a drive and this big Great Dane followed the car up the road. All the other restaurant owners were upset because we opened so early. They didn't know how we sold our scones for the cream teas so cheap, but Bob told them it was because we baked our own and didn't buy them in.

I was very famous for my tea time treats. I was in charge of the salad bar and the tea and Knickerbocker Glory bar. Bob was the cook. We had two waitresses and one washer up and kitchen hand. The girls used to help at weekends and after school. They decided to work all over the school holidays. My friend Maureen's girls came down from London for a working holiday for the summer season. I think all the kids had a lovely time at Riverside. John Dumper and two more of Sean's friends used to help out also. I got so tired because we opened so early and closed so late at night. One night I fell asleep on the toilet and no one could find me.

My sister Jackie, Mum and Uncle Frank came to stay at Christmas. Jackie had a lovely baby Rachael and her boyfriend told us he was going to marry Jackie. We had a bit of a party. Julie, Cathy and Sean went off to the disco followed by lots of other teenagers. I soon got a message from the disco owner telling me Cathy was drunk and disorderly in the toilets. She was only fourteen, so I sent John, Jackie's boyfriend, to collect her. He soon came back and said she tried to kick him in the goolies, so I had to tell Bob and he brought her home. We put her to bed and said she was grounded. The next summer Bob took on a new washer up and kitchen hand. I told him to make sure she was younger than me, because I wanted to be in charge. I was about thirty-nine by then. A big lady came for an interview. She had a limp and a funny eye.

"No way is she working here," I thought, but he gave her the job.

"Bob!" I said, "I told you she must be younger than me!"

"Well, she is five years younger than you," came the reply.

Still, Rosemary was a good worker, apart from the times she was watching the ships come in and all the sailors. Every now and again she was chasing Seán around and giving him foreign cigarettes. She was a bit of a mystery really.

We decided to enter the Carnival celebrations. We all wore blue jeans and white 'T' shirts with Riverside on them. We were all dancing and singing *Down by the Riverside*. We were all rocking and rolling, when suddenly we lost Rosemary, she was carrying a placard with Bed & Breakfast on it. Someone saw her go into a very salubrious pub, but not come out.

from left to right, kitchen maid, Rosemary, Cathy, Seán, Bob, John Dumper, Paul, Julie and Sheila

15

We Lost Rosemary

Rosemary didn't come back to work for three days, after which Bob sacked her. Then Seań told us he thought she was a lady of the night, one of Teignmouth's 'Quay rats'. Well you learn something every day!

My dear old uncle Frank came to stay with us. He really loved Teignmouth and staying at Riverside. He used to go for a little drink most evenings. I think he had a thing for Rosemary. He said there was a very colourful pub by the Quay he wanted to visit. He said it was famous for the beer and was in the good beer guide. I didn't like to tell him it was also famous for something else. I thought, "He is old enough, he will find out for himself!"

Robbie came home on leave from the Army. "See if you can find Uncle Frank," I said. But he couldn't, so when we closed we went out looking for him.

We found him staggering along the road with a smile on his face.

We linked arms and he said he had a lovely time and Rosemary was very attractive with her make- up on. I opened the front door to our hall way and helped Frank along the hall. To my surprise he mounted the ottoman I kept the waitresses pinnies in.

As I held his hand he walked across it and stepped down the other side, I looked at him and said, "And now we will be going up the stairs!" but I think he thought he had already done that.

I was very upset when we were told *Riverside* was to be sold to a property developer company. It was next to a big ship yard, which had been closed for several years. The property developer wanted to build flats on the site. Riverside was such a good business. We had six letting bedrooms from which I did bed & breakfast and it was very popular in town. Bob looked for work when we had to leave Riverside. We were interviewed for licensed premises as Bob said he wanted to run a pub. I wasn't so keen. I had lived in a pub all my life and had always wanted my own home with my own family.

I was so lucky to have two boys and two girls, but I was disappointed because we lived in such a lovely part of the country and couldn't make a living. I didn't want my children leaving home to find work. But now Seán said he was going to London to look for a job. He went to stay with my friend Maureen and her husband Rob. They had four girls all the same age as our family. They lived in Harrow and Seán found a job in a butchers shop where they were going to train him.

16

The End of an Era

"Daddy!" I can remember saying to Daddy, when I was about thirteen years old, "there is a lovely red brick house in Willis Road for sale. It has a tree in the front garden. Why don't you buy it, something to retire to much later on?"

"Oh, Sheila," he said, "an old man died in that house and anyway, people like us can't buy a house. It isn't done."

I really wish he had bought that house. He was so surprised when we bought our house in Lovedean. He was so worried about it, but so proud when he came to visit us when we had our girls christened. We were the first couple to buy our own home in the family.

Alas, Dad died in the George in his bed with Mum looking after him. He worked so hard. They both did. I wish they had taken notice of me and retired to that little house in Willis Road.

It was a very sad time for me. My lovely Daddy had died and Mum was finding it hard to keep the pub going. She had managers to help but nothing worked, so after forty years she gave the pub up and it was sold by the Brewers.

Two chaps, who are actors in East Enders, have bought it, Ricky and Phil Mitchell. The George IV is so different now. Mum said all the bedrooms are bed sitters and they have gaming rooms in the cellar, but I have never been back there. I left there to get married and as a child I saw the walls blown out by the bombs in the war. Why would I want to go back?

My mum took a Council flat in Tufnell Park which she shared with Donald, my Dad's cousin. He had lived at the George all his adult life. It was what they wanted to do.

My mum carried on working in her friend's pub until she was over seventy-five years old. Then she was looking after an old lady for a few years. We made sure she came to visit us every summer and also at Christmas.

The next Christmas my Sister Jackie came to live with us, with her two babies, Rachael was eighteen months old and Lucy was a baby. It was Boxing Day when John her Ex delivered her too us. He went off on his own. She was so depressed it was so sad. We were finding it hard to manage but now we had three more people under our roof. I had a job in a Golf Club and a baby sitting job at a hotel in the evenings. Cathy had a job after school in a wet fish shop.

Bob got a job in Arabia again. We had a house full of children and teenagers. At least I now had a cooker. It was a bit easier, but we had two babies to bath and lots of nappies to wash. It was really hard work with no washing machine and not enough hot water for us all to have a bath. Cathy smelt of fish and Jackie needed a bath, as she had not long had a baby. The Rayburn only gave us enough hot water for one bath a day.

I remember the time my friend Maureen came to stay for the weekend. I was at work, so she stoked up the Rayburn all day and filled a bath for me when I returned from work. "Have your bath and leave the water in for me," she said. "I don't mind using your bath water."

Oh, it was heaven! I wallowed in the soap suds and wrapped myself in a nice warm towel. Then I pulled the plug out. Oh no! What a mistake! How could I tell her what I had done?

Seań was getting on fine in London, John Dumper had now followed him to Harrow. They made a lot of new friends. Sean moved out of Maureen's; her four girls were too much for him, I think. He got himself some nice digs. But I still missed him. He was only eighteen.

Maureen came to stay again for the weekend. It was getting near my fortieth birthday and Bob had organised his leave. He would be home for April 19th.

Seań came home over Easter. He brought six friends with him, some of them had never been to the sea side before. I put up a tent in the garden to give them more room. Jackie and babies had one room Julie, Cathy and now we had Kevin Robbins lodging with us as well. It was getting a bit crowded. Maureen shared a room with me. I was a bit nervous since Bob was away. I had a ghost in my room and she was walking up and down getting nearer to my bed every night. She wore a long grey cloak and always appeared before midnight.

The boys had a lovely holiday. I put a long table and benches in the garden and filled it with homemade bread and sausages. I always made my own bread and pizza. The Rayburn came in useful after all.

Bob didn't come home for my birthday. He didn't phone or let me know why. One month later he still didn't come home. I was getting worried. No letter for weeks, no phone call. I couldn't get in touch with him. We had a pay phone in our house because the kids wouldn't keep away from it. I phoned Maureen.

"Please come back to Devon. I know something is wrong. Something has happened to him."

Maureen arrived on Friday night. We tried to phone Arabia. I kept putting in coins, but it wouldn't work, so I asked my neighbour if I could use her phone and would pay her when her bill came in. She was very understanding. I got through to the compound and spoke to one of his workmen. Bob was the Manager of this division. I asked why he didn't come home two months ago when he had his leave. This chap said another workman had used Bob's leave, but Bob would be home soon.

He couldn't come home now because he was in prison. He had been arrested because he had called in security. Some radio telephones had gone missing. A man who worked in the store had come back to England on Bob's ticket. He told Bob his Mother was dying of cancer and he needed to get home right away. It wasn't until after this worker had gone, that Bob discovered the missing phones.

We waited month after month. I had to get in touch with the Foreign Office in Westminster to find out what they were going to do about it. They said they knew Bob was innocent, but if the other gentleman was to return to Jeddah he would get a hundred flogs and prison for ten years and might not survive it. They had talked to Bob and asked him to sit tight and he would soon be released, but it took so long and my children were so upset. Cathy kept crying.

The newspapers got hold of it and we were all in the papers, even the Sun. I was on TV saying my husband hasn't done anything wrong. I lost so much weight. I was seven stone by now. I was also working in a wine bar. My boss didn't like my weight loss. I thought we would never see Bob again.

Bob's Mum wrote to Margaret Thatcher and got an answer. I wrote to my MP, Maxwell Hyslop. He was no help; he said my husband shouldn't work in another country. I was at my wit's end. We had no money for months. The Social Services didn't know how to treat me, so they decided to deal with my family as if my husband was dead.

17

Bob Lost in Arabia

I kept ringing Westminster.

I got friendly with the secretary of the person in charge of Bob's case. She often phoned me at home in the evening and let me know what was happening. She said he was okay. He was fit and well and was not ill treated. He shared a cell with thirty other people, Arabs, one Canadian, one Englishman, several Philippians and Koreans. The men he worked with took food in to him every day because they don't feed you in jail in Arabia. She didn't know when he would be released, but he had been to court and found not guilty. Now he was waiting for his passport to be given back to him. He had to pay his own fare and had no money, so the chaps at work paid it out of his wages that should have gone to me. They had been hanging on to it for months.

Maureen and I demolished several wood sheds we had in the gardens and we used them as fuel for the Rayburn as we couldn't afford coal.

"Do you think Bob will notice the sheds have gone when he gets home?" I said one day.

No one told me when Bob was due home. I knew it must be soon. I wanted to meet him at the airport at Heathrow. Westminster said he was coming home at the weekend so I got the night train to London. The Arabian flight arrived about six in the morning, but he wasn't on it.

I went to London six times, sometimes staying overnight at Maureen's because she lived near the airport. Late one night I got a phone call from a Canadian chap who said Bob would be released within the next few days. He said he had been sharing a cell with Bob and they looked out for each other. He said Bob was in good spirits.

The next weekend he did come home. He arrived at the airport before me. Maureen said her husband, Rob, had met him and they were sitting in the café with a bottle of wine. I think I was thinner than him! I expect it was all that rice he had eaten every day. He didn't say much about his treatment, but we did discover he had been tortured. But at least it was all over now.

Seań came back home on holiday and Robbie. We had a family party and Bob and I were on TV and Cathy stopped crying.

Robbie was out of the Army and had a job. He got engaged to Paula and a wedding was arranged.

I landed a nice job with the Council as Receptionist at Dawlish Swimming Pool and Bob started up his own plumbing and electrical business, but we had to put the house up for sale. My sister Jackie and babies went back to London, as she got control of her old house and wanted to go to college and get her life on track.

Our son Robbie got married to Paula in May. They had a small reception on the river. My mum and Auntie Mary came to Dawlish and it was a very happy time.

Cathy and Kevin were an item, also Julie and Chris. Soon Robbie and Paula had a little son who they called Liam. I often wonder if Robbie wanted him called Liam after that little Irish baby I looked after so many years ago, because that baby grew up and used to follow me everywhere. When we moved to Lovedean he came to visit me with an army convoy of tanks which took up most of the road. Robbie was only little, but he was in awe of Liam. Liam had joined the Army and brought several soldiers to my front door for sausage sandwiches. All the neighbours must have wondered what all the tanks were doing! Had war broken out in Lovedean Lane.

Cathy and Kevin were expecting a baby. It was soon our 25th Wedding Anniversary and we had organised a party in the football club for the Saturday. But on the previous Thursday, the 6th of August, we were having a drink in our local pub in the village to celebrate, when Cathy went into labour. We rushed her to hospital, and she had a lovely little girl called "Sihona" and on the Saturday she brought her to the party to show her off to all our relations. My Mum, Bob's Mum and Dad and all my sisters and cousins were there also. Maureen came from Harrow.

That weekend we discovered that Seań wasn't at all well. He said he had an appointment at Mount Vernon Hospital when he got back to London, so I said I would go up to London for the weekend and stay with Maureen and then go with him to his appointment, because I was worried about him.

It was really bad news.

Poor Seań had Hodgkin's disease, cancer of the lymph gland, and had to have chemo therapy and radium. His firm gave him three months leave and I arranged with the hospital for him to have his treatment at home in Dawlish. The consultant said she would arrange it with Exeter Hospital.

Seań was only nineteen.

He was in a band and all his friends rallied around him. John Dumper took Seań's place in the band because his singing voice was very good. He even sang *Love me Tender* at our 25th Party!

Seań had to spend some time in Mount Vernon Hospital before coming home. His mates were always around his bed. They joked about putting his sperm in the sperm bank and picked out a nice nurse to help him, but the consultant thought he might be OK and not have to do that.

After Seań's treatment he went back to London. The hospital helped him to get his own flat in Pinner. It really was nice. I helped him furnish it and made curtains. John Dumper wanted to move in with him, but now Seań had a girl friend called Andria so she moved in with him instead.

Well, it wasn't long before Andrea became pregnant and Oliver Ben was born. Seań was over the moon because he knew now he could father a child, and this one was very special. Ollie had olive skin and dark brown eyes and tight curly hair, and when they came to visit us in Devon he played with his cousins and they were very happy times. Seań and Andrea started looking for a little house to buy in Wales, and soon found something that suited them. Ollie was two by this time.

Arabian Homecoming – Bob and Sheila

18

Hooray, My Sister is Back

My Sister Jackie moved back to Devon and got a flat in Teignmouth. She now attended the University of Exeter as she wanted to qualify as a Probation Officer. Her girls went to the same local school "Our Lady and St Patrick" that Cathy had attended. It was nice to have my little sister living near me again.

We moved from Holcombe to Dawlish and this time bought a town house next door to a Chinese Takeaway and opposite a pub. The house was Bob's choice it had a big old barn on the back which was falling down, and a hundred foot garden. It was a good spot for trading and Bob was so busy with his central heating orders, because I only worked Sunday, Monday and Tuesday. I helped Cathy look after her baby so she could do a little job Wednesday, Thursday and Friday. It worked out very well. Cathy and Kevin had a nice little flat in Dawlish. Julie and Chris moved in together and bought a house in Kingsteignton. Chris trained to be a barber and now he had his own shop. Julie had a very good job with the Ministry of Defence and was moving up the promotion ladder. My sister Maureen's son, Paul, married and we all went to the wedding in Essex.

It was lovely for all the family to get together again.

Seań was now in remission. He loved his flat in Pinner, and Andrea, his girl friend. Cathy's second child, Zara was born in May. She was a lovely child. I looked after both girls for Cathy and enjoyed it very much. Zara was a very intelligent child and had a very infectious laugh.

One terrible Sunday morning I got a phone call to say Zara had been found dead from the Cot Death Syndrome.

My poor Cathy and Kevin were in pieces.

How would they get over it? All the family were in complete shock. Seań was very upset. Robbie and his wife Paula were devastated. Their little boy and girl, Stephanie, missed the baby so much. Julie and Chris were very supportive of Cathy and Kevin.

My poor daughter! Losing a child is something one never gets over.

Seań and Andrea were not getting on too well. Seań loved Andrea but she found herself another boy friend and she moved him into the house they had bought in Wales. I asked Cathy to go and visit Seań and see if he wanted to come home to tell him he would be welcome. After four weeks Seań came home. He said Andrea's boy friend was very good with Ollie and as long as they paid the mortgage they could have the house.

Seań got a butcher's job in Shaldon and was getting on OK, then one day a few weeks later, Andrea's boy friend arrived with Ollie. He said Andrea was in trouble with the Police, so could we look after Ollie?

Seań was very pleased to see him, but he was so thin and had lots of warts all over hands. We got him checked out. The doctor said he was under nourished. It took a long time to get Ollie on to good food, but Seań was a good cook and it wasn't long before Ollie was back to normal.

Seań took a part time job to spend more time with Ollie and we got him into a nursery school. Time went by and we got in touch with Andrea. Seań kept asking when she was coming for Ollie. But by this time she had lost the house and moved back to London. She didn't want to come for her little boy. Ollie loved his nursery. I hoped she would come before he started school.

We used to take the children and grand children to Barry Island for a cheap holiday camp holiday. My sister and her girls came. We used to have a great time and enter into all the competitions. I won the Glamorous Granny competition and we all got a free holiday for the next year. Then I won the best dressed lady! We had several holidays there until the camp closed down and Seań and Ollie used to really enjoy it.

We were making plans for Julie and Chris to get married. It would be a big affair. I made her gown from Oyster silk with antique lace trimming. She looked stunning. My sister Jackie's two daughters were flower girls and grand daughters, Sihona and Stephanie, were bride's maids. Cathy was Julie's chief bride's maid and young Liam looked so cute in his tail suit. Ollie was the youngest in a little Sailor suit, Seán and Robbie, Chris and Kevin looked great in their tail suits. It was a great occasion.

The next year it was Cathy's turn and we arranged a reception in the local Manor House. Mum came to Devon and we looked for a gown for Cathy. I wanted to make it, but Cathy said I could do the flower girl dresses. Cathy chose a black satin gown with white appliqué on the bodice. She looked wonderful, but I was worried because it was very very black. Mum was very cheeky to encourage her to buy it. It was going to be a big surprise to all the family. I made the bride's maid's dresses in silver grey satin with black sashes. Ollie wore a suit with a bow tie. All the men looked smart with silver grey ties and striped trousers. Kevin was in black and white. On the morning of the wedding Cathy descended the staircase in our cottage looking just such a picture.

Bob looked up the stairs at his daughter and said, "Oh! Give me a brandy, quick!"

Everything went off so well. They had a white super stretch limousine which really showed off the black satin gown.

19

My dream Comes True at Last

That year I opened my own shop in Dawlish and called it

Wouldn't it be lovely

I had got my shop at last!

We changed our living room into a show room and moved ourselves to the back of the house. Now we needed to start work on the old barn and build it into a home for ourselves.

To promote my little shop I dressed in a beautiful full length silk gown and blonde wig. I stood in the window of my friend's printing shop. It was April 1st and I was a mannequin. The Gazette newspaper photographer stood by to take photos of people's reactions when I winked at them as they passed the shop. The school children were taken by surprise and loved the joke. One poor old man pranged his car and the fender fell off.

Swift Print offered me their mannequin for my new shop. I duly collected it the next day, dressed as a gorilla!

I flashed through the shop door and proceeded to move the mannequin, but it was rather heavy, so I had to take the arms off first and then the torso and the legs. I had to run down the road and put each limb in the car which was waiting. I had arms and legs sticking out of windows. My daughter-in-law, Paula, was driving and grand daughter Stephanie, aged six, said, "Hurry up, nanny."

Wow how did she know it was me in that outfit?

The Gazette was waiting and more photos were taken for the local newspaper.

Bob re-mortgaged the house and along with two other builders we built a lovely new house.

It would be time for Ollie to start school the next summer and Andrea still hadn't come for him, so Seań decided to go for custody of him. Seań wasn't at all well, but Andrea insisted the case was held in London. It was a lot of travelling for Seań.

He had a check up and to our horror we discovered the cancer had returned. More chemo and radium treatment. How much could he stand! Still, he took Ollie to school every morning, although he looked so frail. The Judge gave Seań a Residency Order on Ollie until he was eighteen, and we all took each day as it came.

Seań attended all Ollie's school functions and sports days. Seań and Ollie were allocated a lovely new house near his school. Seań painted all the rooms in pastel colours.

It was looking very nice and in a good position for a Housing Association house. They had lovely neighbours. All the children in the road used to play together. But I was very worried about Seań. He was very sick. The next day his neighbour phoned and said he had taken Ollie to school for Seań as he wasn't well, could I get up to the house right away? I couldn't find Bob he was at work, but I didn't know where.

Opening of *Wouldn't it be Lovely* – Sheila, model and James Wright

20

My Worst Fears Become Reality

We got Seań into hospital. Hours later I got hold of Bob and he came to the hospital, but it was too late.

Seań had passed away.

I seemed to be struck dumb. Cathy and Kevin arrived at the hospital.

It was the worst day of my life.

How would we tell Ollie? How would we cope? Ollie stayed with neighbours over night and the next day Cathy broke the news to him. He cried and cried. He was only six.

"How do I pay the rent?" he said.

Bob and I were to be Ollie's new parents. The whole family were devastated by the news. His friends in London were heart broken and John Dumper and all his band of Rockabillies came for his funeral and we continued to take one day at a time. We loved Ollie and did our best by him.

It changed my life.

On the first summer term after Seań's death, it was me who attended Ollie's Sports Day. I always loved the kids Sports Day and used to go with Seań to cheer Ollie and his team on.

But that year when Ollie was seven I was on my own and sat with other Mothers. All his class mates encouraged me to enter the Mother's sprint race. Oh my goodness, I couldn't let him down. As I was running my hardest I could hear them all shouting,

"Come on, Nan! Come on, Nan!"

All his pals called me Nan and I rather liked that. I encouraged him to invite members of his class to have a sleep- over. I didn't want him to be any different from them.

Getting back to the race, I came second from last, not as good as Princess Diana, but after all I *am* a grandmother!

One day after school Ollie whispered in my ear, "Can Rachael and Rebecca have a sleep- over with us this weekend?"

I couldn't really understand who he wanted; I thought he said Keith and Robbie. I kept asking him if it was two boys? He got a bit ruffled and said,

"They are twins."

I said, "OK who are they?"

Then I understood he meant two girls. I turned to the Headmaster,

"Do you think it is okay?"

"Oh come, Mrs Thomas, they are innocent children."

So the girls slept over in sleeping bags in Ollie's room and the next morning they came down the stairs on their bottoms in their sleeping bags for their breakfast pancakes. The twins were Ollie's best friends for many years.

Ollie seemed to play the video of *The Lion King* all the time. He said his Daddy had said it was a good story and he should play it over and he would learn a lot by it. Bob said, "Seań wanted us to bring Ollie up if anything happened to him."

We got custody of Ollie. The Judge gave us the Residency Order until he was eighteen. We didn't hear from or see Andrea. We couldn't find her to tell her the news, but she did phone after six months. Her Mother said they were so sorry and that they liked Seań so much and were ashamed of the way Andrea treated him and Ollie.

John Dumper came to visit Ollie. John's brother David had died from a heart attack at the age of thirty and John came home for his funeral. He said his Mum was heart-broken and would I keep my eye on her since she only lived over the road. So Pat Dumper and I became friends. Now we were both sixty and got a little pension. We were determined to keep young. Pat and I took Ollie ice-skating and swimming in Plymouth. We saved up and took him to the USA when he was twelve. We loved Florida, the theme parks and the film studios and the Wet and Wild parks. We had the time of our lives. Bob had a bad back and found it hard to walk far so he didn't want to come to America.

One year Mum came on holiday with her friend Hilda. As I was busy that day they went off to Exeter to look at the shops and have a bit of lunch. They visited the Cathedral and popped into a little hotel on the green for a little tipple and were greeted in the foyer by a tray of wine, sitting themselves down and watching the world go round. They were offered a second glass which they accepted to their delight. Suddenly a well dressed lady sat beside my mum and said, "How nice to see you. Are you enjoying the wine?"

" Oh, Yes," said mother, "how hospitable of you."

"Well," said the lady, "and what side of the family are you on, the Bride or the Groom's?" after which mum and Hilda made a hasty retreat!

The next year was my sixtieth birthday and mum came to stay. I was having a big party and all my sisters and relatives were invited and that was the year that Bob and I had just started to foster young boys who were on remand and needed a home for various reasons. We thought we could make a difference to their lives.

We had Lee staying with us, a good looking young lad who had been in and out of trouble, but was very likeable. One morning I told Mum I had to pop out to the shops and asked her to keep Lee company. He said he would make her a cup of tea, so I left them chatting away. When I returned mum said he was good company and he had told her his life story. He said he had been in trouble but was misunderstood. She told him I had been a bad girl for driving a car without passing my test. I was flabbergasted and told Mum that with that information she gave him he could blackmail me. "

"He isn't a thief, so you don't have to carry your handbag about with you, but he does steal cars."

"Oh Sheila," she said, "What about your party tonight? Everyone has big cars. Your sister has a Porche. Will it be safe?"

"I don't think so, Mum. That's why I have a Probation Officer come to babysit Lee." A year or so passed and Lee came to visit us after reform school. He asked after Mum, and said, "Is Gran still carrying her handbag under her arm?"

21

Now - Something to Smile About

One day Julie and Chris came over for dinner and broke the news that Julie was pregnant. We were so pleased since we really had given up hope of them having a family. Julie had such a good job and Chris had lots of animals -a zoo more like. They had a lovely house and it wasn't too far away for us to visit on Sundays. Chris's parents lived not far away from them in Ogwell. As Chris's Dad, Brian, was retired from the Police he offered to help with the baby when it arrived, which would mean Julie could return to work with the help of the nursery attached to her firm.

Bethany Lauren arrived in April and five years later Megan Alice came along. Julie and Chris made great parents and moved into a bigger house in Ogwell. The girls were full of life and very beautiful. As they got older they were both keen to model for me in my fashion shows and were a great hit with my clients.

They both had swimming lessons and belonged to Stagecoach Drama Group, so Julie had her time cut out at weekends taking them around.

When Ollie was fifteen, Pat and I took him to New York for Christmas Shopping. Cathy's best friend lives in New York with her husband Baz. He is a tattooist and wanted to do one on Pat and me, but we declined his offer. They took us out most evenings and gave us a great time. One night when we got back to the hotel on Broadway, I said to Pat, "You can't go to bed. It's only midnight and New York never sleeps!"

So I took my tap dancing shoes out of the wardrobe and we both went down to the next block, which was 42nd Street. I did a tap dance on the corner just as a yellow cab was going by. There was a young girl with a camera taking photos and developing them. Pat told her she shouldn't be out so late.

Ollie's school friend met him at the hotel the next day and they went off to a Basket Ball game in Madison Square Gardens. Ollie is very tall and people thought he was one of the players.

Ollie was to leave school when he was sixteen and he applied to Exeter College. He was so good at IT. I really thought his career was in computers. But he did several courses in college in Exeter and still didn't know what he wanted to do.

Our Carnivals in Dawlish were very spectacular. We even had displays by the Red Arrow teams and thousands of people descended on Dawlish in August. I entered the Carnival with a float to advertise my shop and we won the cup for the most decorative float. I put on fashion shows and gave talks to women's's' clubs and I gave a talk on the radio about my days at Norman Hartnell's

On our 40th Anniversary Bob asked me what present I would like.

"Let's have a party and fireworks, lots of big fireworks," I said My son-in-laws liked displays so they helped Bob and we had a great celebration in the garden.

One year I helped the local pub put on a float for the Carnival. We all dressed up as gorillas. I hired the suit for over a week and also used it to wear for my cousin Patrick's 70th birthday. I decided to do a Stripper Gram as a gorilla. I wore a red bra and suspender belt on my hairy body. It was a bit hot inside that outfit and when the music started I did my little dance around Patrick. He had a good sense of fun, but looked a little shocked, so I whispered in his ear,

"Its OK Patrick, its only me, its Sheila,"

But of course in this monkey mask I sounded a bit muffled and anyhow I didn't know that Patrick had gone deaf. He thought I was a real stripper and was going to take the gorilla outfit off and show all my undies, so he pulled my head off. I didn't really want all the family to know it was me. But now they did!

It was coming up to my Granddaughter Sihona's birthday and we all went out for a family meal. Cathy and Sihona were having a teenage party in a pub in Teignmouth on the Saturday.   Only people under eighteen were invited. So Pat and I decided to gate crash it for a joke. We dressed up as Bikers in leather skirts and jackets and long black wigs and hats and chains. We took a bottle of Champagne for Si and her chums. The door man let us in, but Cathy chucked us out. It's the first time I've been banned.

It was a long time before Cathy forgave us!

Our Son- in- law broke his leg. He had a motor bike accident. When the children got home from school Julie broke the news to them because Chris would have a caste on his leg.

"Daddy has had a little accident," she said,

"Oh!" said Megan. "Has he wet the bed?"

I called my Granddaughter Bessy Baggage and the youngest Magic Meg. They are lovely girls.

I was commissioned to make a 1950's wedding gown for a young lady from Bath. She was getting wed in Las Vegas USA in a Chapel of Elvis Presley. The dress was pink and black with loads of petticoats. She was delighted with the finished result.

Bob and I were invited to Bath when they got back from the USA. A big party was put on in the assembly rooms in the Bath hotel. Bob and I danced to a band called "The Perfectly Frank". The singer looked like Frank Sinatra and sang like him too. Bob thought he was great.

We had a wonderful time.

22

Dawlish Calendar Girls

Pat and I had just seen the film Calendar Girls and I thought it would be a good idea to promote my shop and Dawlish if we did a calendar ourselves. There were several ladies of a certain age who like me ran their own business. I contacted them to see if they were up for it, but all in the best possible taste. I said we would put Dawlish on the map. We are not all fuddy duddies!

I enrolled a lady photographer and our all lady team were ready. My photo shoot would be shot in my own shop, in front of my own lovely big mirror.

I wrapped myself in a yard of blue satin and just a pair of lace hold- up stockings. The photographer arrived. I put on a dressing gown and opened the door for her, but she insisted I helped her carry the lights out of her car.

As I reached her car my Chinese neighbour caught me, and said looking down at my ankles, "Oh Sheila, you look lovely!"

To my horror, one of my stockings was hanging down! Never mind, the photos were really good.

We had a lot of fun doing the calendar. Each lady promoted her own shop, from the hairdresser to the florist, to the pub landlady, who, by the way, had lots of letters from soldiers serving abroad. They made her their pin up!

Carnival week was a busy time in Dawlish and bunting was hung all over town, except in our street. We did have some one year. I actually had to beg for it and the Council gave us some, but it was stolen and they wouldn't give us any more. So I decided to make our own. I used the finest silks and satins I had over from the gowns I had made. They were very vibrant colours. I got a bit bored cutting out triangles, so cut some in the shape of knickers and panties. I added lace on the legs. When we hung them up they looked great. It took a bit of time before people noticed the odd pair of panties, then they started to count how many they could see. It certainly brought a lot of people up to the top of the town. They came in groups and were having bets on how many knickers they could spot.

The radio got to hear about it, and the papers, and I ended up on TV. I was famous for a short while.

My business was going well. The prom gowns I received from the USA were very popular. I didn't order two the same, so the girls were thrilled to have something different from the usual off the peg gown.

The fashion shows took a lot of organising. One of my clients had a big hotel overlooking the sea. She said we could hold our fashion shows there. Her staff put up a nice catwalk and friends rallied around to help out. My models were models from the 6th form secondary school and the hairdressers. I even encouraged four local men to model and we all enjoyed it.

We gave each customer a glass of wine, held a raffle, and had a professional singer to perform. We made a little profit, but the main purpose was to promote my shop. The local papers were standing by and took loads of photographs, which were eventually printed in a local magazine.

To promote my shop, I was also asked to do a photo shoot in a beautiful manor house for a new Devon Magazine. I picked six models and six lovely gowns, three of which were my own designs, and three wedding dresses from America, which were very elaborate and had just come out on the market. Everything went very well and it was a great promotion for my shop.

Everyone liked the name of my little shop, but little did they know I had to call it *Wouldn't it be Lovely* because Mr Hartnell had said that to me many years ago when I discussed my wedding gown with him. We came to a decision on the design and he had said, "Oh, wouldn't it be lovely!"

Although my shop was small it really was lovely, with a big mirror on the main wall where the ingle nook fireplace used to be. I swathed the mirror with a garland of roses and leaves around the frame. It looked very fairy-like. I had some lovely open wardrobes made all around the walls in white, with dark green pelmets edged in gold and all my gowns hung on white satin hangers. It was my little Hartnell's for over fifteen years and I was a one-woman business.

My husband hadn't been too well lately, so we decided to wind our business down and sell our house, then plan the next part of our lives. Oliver had finished at college and was applying for jobs in the car trade. I insisted he got a part time job and saved up for a car. On his seventeenth birthday I treated him to driving lessons, but how was I to know it would take him almost a year to pass his test?

Ollie got a part time job as a waiter in The Ugly Duckling. He was enjoying it, but got so tall his head was hitting the ceiling lights as he carried the plates to the table. He got quite good at ducking. Then he got an evening job at the Langstone Cliff Hotel to boost his earnings. At last he had enough for a car. Julie's husband went with him to view an old car. It was a Rover and okay for a first car and at last he passed his test.

Ollie applied for lots of jobs and at last was taken on by the Police to do an apprenticeship in car body work. They have also put him in for an advanced driving test and as a Police driver.

For his eighteenth birthday Ollie and several of his old school friends went to Ayainapa in Cyprus for two weeks. He said it was the first holiday without his family and I think they had a great time.

Sheila Thomas

Sheila Thomas's

Wouldn't it be Lovely

Bridalwear Shop
also Ball Gowns
Tiaras and
Accessories

3 King Street
Dawlish
Devon
01626 863881

......Open 10am to 5pm Tuesday to Saturday

APRIL 2005

Mon	Tue	Wed	Thu	Fri	Sat	Sun
				1	2	3
4	5	6	7	8	9	10
11	12	13	14	15	16	17
18	19	20	21	22	23	24
25	26	27	28	29	30	

Sheila - Miss April

23

My Dream has Ended

It is 2006 and I have just closed my shop door for the last time. It is Christmas and my Mother is staying in Okehampton with my sister Jackie and her daughters. I have invited her to come and stay with us for the New Year. I have made an appointment for my Mum and me to have our hair done at the hairdresser's down the road. I have booked tickets for a New Year Party at the local Holiday Camp. Julie, Chris and the children are to join us, also Cathy, Kevin and Sihona. We are all looking forward to it. I have also invited Pat Dumper as she is on her own for New Year. We have two big Christmas trees up outside the shop and coloured lights.

It will be the last time.

I have booked for us all to go to the Pantomime in our local theatre in Dawlish. Mum said she was really looking forward to it.

The day before New Year's Eve Mum arrived. My sister Jackie's future son -in -law delivers her. It was lovely to see Mum again. My Son Robbie arrived and we all had a cup of coffee, but Mum didn't seem to be very well, although she insisted she was okay.

We sat around chatting before going to bed and the next day, New Year's Eve, we took a short walk to the hairdressers. Mum knew the girl who does her hair when she comes on holiday; they caught up with all the news! We booked a taxi for the evening party and it went very well. At the end of the night we wished each other a Happy New Year and made our way home.

Mum woke up at five in the morning and was wandering around. She insisted on getting dressed, but then slept in the chair in front of the TV all morning. We were invited to go to Julie and Chris's for tea that afternoon. Mum said she felt okay, but I was so worried about her, she seemed very strange. We didn't stay with Julie too long. I could see that my Mum was very ill. The next day my doctor checked Mum over and said we must get her home right away. Chris and Bob drove her back to London where my sister Patricia was waiting to look after her for a week.

We discovered that Mum had had a stroke and then another one when she was in hospital. I was due to start a job in a rather posh Bridal Shop in Exeter. I wasn't feeling at all well. I had a bad cold and was very depressed. I couldn't stop thinking about my poor old Mum.

My two daughters made me laugh relating stories to me about a holiday they had with my mother at the George when they were aged twelve and fourteen. They said she took them up the West End in a taxi. No buses for my old mum! Firstly, she raided her safe and took out several bags of fifty pence pieces. She took them to

Selfridges and had their ears pierced, and their lovely long hair cut into a bob. Then off for knickerbocker glories in the ice cream parlour and on to the Palladium for a show and surprise, surprise, a taxi home. It seems this little trip happened a few times. I think my mum's handbag must have been very heavy, because I remember having such happy trips to the West End with Mum as a girl.

Christmas 2006 and New Year 2007 was one of the worst times of my life. My dream ended, my shop was closed and my poor old mum was fading away.

If I don't write this book now at the age of 69, I may one day end up with alzheimers and loose my memories of a lifetime.

My Mum had vascular dementure the last few years of her life resulting from several strokes. There were many things she forgot. She once tried to tell me I wasn't evacuated to Essex during the war for six years to live with my grandmother. She said I only went to visit on the odd occasion. I was so upset, I argued as I knew this was not the case.

I had so many memories and I felt that my Mum was trying to rub them out. Now I know my dear old Mum couldn't help it, but all the same it hurt. So you see - I have to write this now while it's fresh in my mind.

If I don't do it now I will never do it. I won't have the patience or the inclination.

This book is a true story. There is a lot more about the George I could write about, but my three sisters would not be happy. They are a lot younger than me. My youngest sibling is seventeen years younger.

They would not believe the half of it. They would think I was making it up. But they would believe the other half and want it kept secret.

The seedy side of the George will be kept secret by me as some of the people it involved are still around. But my dear friend Doreen and I know the truth because she was there also and we often talk about it. But that is another book that will never get written.

I had slowly been noticing the change in my mum as for years she stayed with me in Devon for a summer holidays, for two weeks in August. I suppose I noticed it more because she was so close to me for long periods. When she stayed with my sister in Essex it was only for a few days at a time, and she was on her best behaviour. You would hardly notice the little signs.

The physical deterioration was evident to me. The mental deterioration was devastating to me. She slept for hours during the day, and if she had a forgetful moment she would say, "Oh what a silly girl I am."

She would get all her times mixed up and would be walking around at five in the morning to go to the toilet and forget where her bedroom was and attempt to go into my grandson's bedroom and insist it was her room and I must have moved it.

All this happened one year before she died. She didn't seem to be able to see half the time, although insisting she could. She was staying with my youngest sister in Okehampton for Christmas, but would phone me at seven in the morning saying everyone was in bed and she was on her own. She misdialled and thought she was phoning her boyfriend. She stayed with me in the New Year and was so confused, putting on her make up and getting dressed at five in the morning. She dropped a big dressing table mirror.

I rushed to her room, "Oh, please mum, go back to bed. I am so tired." I said. I knew then that I couldn't look after her if it really came to it. She needed full time care.

We all know much of the disease's cruel capacity to confuse and disorientate, to erase from elderly minds the multitude of memories that link them to the past. We know how it changes loved ones into strangers and robs sufferers of personality and identity.

Everything I have ever seen about dementia was so miserable. She told me at a wedding that my middle sister whom I had just been talking to had gone off crying. Had I upset her? It was not true. I looked for my sister, found her and asked, "Are you okay?"

Smiling, she said, "Yes of course I'm okay. I am having a cigarette outside."

Oh Mum, how your mind is so muddled. I needed my mum to be safe, but she said a care home was out of the question. So my sister Jackie took control as she was in the best position to do so. She sold my mother's flat and bought a big house between them. A new start for Gladys which only lasted five months. It was so sad.

My Mother died in February 2008 and as I stood at my Mother's graveside, the sun was shining and I remembered my Father and the day he was buried.

Now I am burying my Mother, as my Mother's coffin was lowered into the ground to be with my Father, I threw a handful of earth on to the coffin and thought,

"Goodbye, Duchess. This is the end of an era."

Model Marilyn Adams and Sheila in the Manor house.

Epilogue

I had to write this book now for my grandchildren and great grandchildren that may come along. I want them to know all about the past from 1939, my upbringing in the George IV in North London, and my parents. There will never be another World War 2. There will never be another Gladys and John who helped so many Irish relations and took nothing in return.

There will never be another Norman Hartnell who trained so many young girls to make Coronation gowns and Wedding gowns for Queen Elizabeth and many other famous people. That way of life is no more and I think there will never be another Sheila Thomas nee Dowling.

Since my mother's death, I have been driven to get my book published. She gave me lots of information to help me move on with the stories. She told me the things about my granddad, Charlie South. Oh, how she must have loved him!

Well, my shop closed in 2006, and after a short interlude in the bridal shop in Exeter I took stock of my life. "What do I want to do? "Who will take me on at my age?" were just two of the questions buzzing round my head. I like meeting people. I'm a bubbly person. It would be fun to work at a funfair or even a circus, but I'm not that good at heights or even going around fast in circles.

I take a walk along the seafront in Teignmouth. The sea looks lovely, the sun is shining and the music is ringing out from the Pier. There is a big notice in the window;

Seasonal Staff wanted.

"Wow, if I can't get a job in the circus or the funfair, The Pier is the next best thing, I will try my luck," I said to myself.

A lovely lady called Lucie gave me an interview. "You will be ideal for running the gift shop," she said. And so I started working five days a week on The Grand Pier at Teignmouth.

It was only fifteen minutes away from my home and, since I have a bus pass, my fare is free. There are some advantages to being over sixty!

At the end of October The Pier is closed. Oh, I missed the fun. "I'll try my luck now at being a City Girl," I thought. So I took myself off to Exeter. All those lovely new shops, they must need a person like me! All the shop assistants looked so young and trendy. Where will I fit in? *Make a Bear Shop* looked good fun! Tell the little kiddies a story while you make and stuff a teddy of their choice, put a little heart inside and a voice message – just the job over Christmas time. But not for me! Sadly.

Strolling through Exeter I noticed a card in *Evans'* shop window; fashion advisor wanted for the Christmas and January period. That's for me! I filled in the application form and handed in my C.V. The interview was the next day. Time to make myself look smart. – neat jacket and skirt, high heels, bit more red to my hair, Estee Lauder makeup and I was set.

A sweet girl called Lydia interviewed me. "You will be ideal," she said. "But you didn't put your date of birth on the form." "Does it matter?" says I. "Not really," said Lydia. We have a lady of sixty-five working here." "Oh, really!" I said with a smile, "Well, I am younger than Joan Collins but older than the lady who works here."

I got the job!

The girls there were really lovely – both young and old. The manager, Karen, was very nice. She had to smile when I advised a young man who wanted a dress for his new year party. I helped him into a flowery number and then suggested black lace leggings and red high heeled shoes.

On January 20th my *Evans* job finished, but I was back on The Pier by March again – back to t-shirt, jeans and trainers. How time flies.

This is the third year on the Pier for me and now the season is over again and Lydia has phoned me, wanting me back at *Evans* for November. But I thought it was time for a rest, time to spend with my husband and get on with my book.

In between my jobs we turned my shop into a holiday cottage, my husband decorated it throughout. We had great fun furnishing it. I made brochures and our grandson created a lovely website, and we called it *Little Mermaid Cottage.*

Now it is 2010 and we are looking forward to our fiftieth Wedding Anniversary. We are having a big party and I will invite Susan from Poland.

I met Susan while I was working on the Pier. She told me she was writing a book set in Teignmouth. I told her I had written a book but couldn't find an agent and didn't know what to do next. What a co-incidence. Su has the same initials as me - S.M.T. - Susan Mary Thomas. It must be an omen! Su has helped me to get my book published at last.

God Bless Susan.

Acknowledgements

Sincere thanks to Patricia Dumper, for without her help the book would never have been written.

With thanks to my grandson Oliver Ben Thomas who has lived with me from the age of three and whom I dearly love - for his advice on computers and his encouragement.

Also Susan Thomas-Czarnecki.

About the Author

Born in war torn London, educated in a convent and couturier for the British Royal family, Sheila Thomas opted out of society, moving to Devon to live the good life as market gardener and greengrocer with her husband Bob.

Finding no money in lettuces, Sheila returned to her seamstress skills; her dreams fulfilled when she opened her very own Bridal Boutique "Wouldn't it be Lovely" in Dawlish, where the black swans live.

Sheila still lives with her husband in Dawlish, spoiling her six grandchildren and getting ready for her Golden Wedding Anniversary.

Lightning Source UK Ltd.
Milton Keynes UK
UKOW02f2136120916

282826UK00001B/9/P